The Saxons

The Story of the Saxon, Henry of Wettin, Coberg and The Pioneer Summerour Family in Founding America

by Susan Moore Teller

Publisher: Lulu Press, Inc. and Susan Moore Teller
February 26 2020

Teller-Moore Associates
PO Box 2484 Sun City AZ 85372-2484
(623)875-0613
Perfect Bound Full Color Paperback
Copyright February 26, 2020 by Susan Moore Teller
ISBN 978-1-67817-417-0

Table of Contents

- The Saxons 3
  - Prologue: 3
  - The Summerour Line 3
    - Henry was a Saxon from Coberg, now Germany 3
    - Henry was in favor of the American Revolution, a Patriot 4
  - 1741 Henry Whitener/Weidner, now 24, came to Philadelphia, Pennsylvania 5
  - Henry Summeour -- from Bavaria to Pennsylvania 5
  - Elizabeth Whitener, daughter of Henry the Saxon, marries Henry Summerour II 6
  - Elizabeth's Grandson is a Goldminer, Strikes it Rich in California 6
  - John Summerour Goes to Georgia-and the Civil War Descends 7
  - Margaret Berry, wife of John Summerour 8
  - the Wininger Connection 12
  - Hickory, North Carolina June 13, 1894 – 16
  - Henry The Saxon Pioneers North Carolina 20
  - King's Mountain with Henry's Musket 22
  - Henry Weidner's Will 23
  - The Descendants of the German Pioneers to North Carolina 27
  - This Authors Proven Direct Line of Descent from Henry Whitner PS, NC and Henry Summerour, Militia, NC 27
  - Professor Deal, docent at Kings Mountain National Park 27
- Two Reports of Some Descendants of the German Pioneers to North Carolina 27
  - 27

The Saxons

By Susan Moore Teller: sm0634@gmail.com

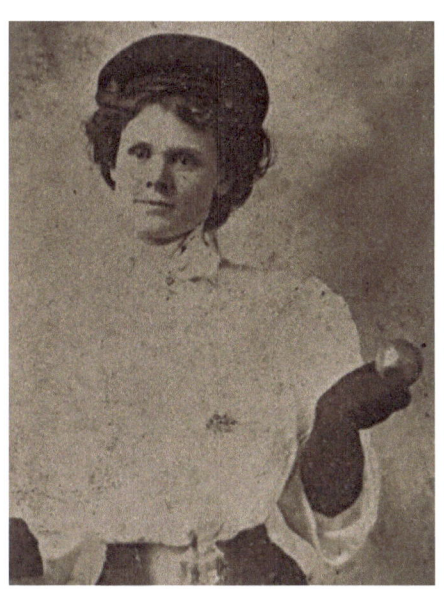

Prologue:
This is the story of Susan Mae Summerour (1859GA-1926TX), her 2nd husband, Porter Kalvin Wininger (1855TN-1951TX) and three of their Wininger daughters who married Moore brothers in early Texas. Her photo was taken at the time of her marriage at age twenty-five to Porter Kalvin Wininger, a widower.

The Summerour Line

Lela Elizabeth Wininger, this writer's grandmother, was the daughter-in-law of Enoch and Susan (Hines) Moore, and the daughter of Porter Kalvin and Susan Mae (Summerour) Wininger. Porter (or PK) and Susie owned a farm in nearby Montague County, in the Red River Valley region bordering Oklahoma. Three of their four daughters married sons of Enoch and Susan. Porter and Susan both were predominantly German in heritage; Porter also said to be ¼ Cherokee via his mother, Nancy Ann Powell; Susan, some Scotch-Irish and English, and also a little Cherokee according to a Georgia descendant on the Summerour "Dillard" line. Germans immigrants were common early in the nation's history. When the nation became sovereign a vote was taken to determine which of the many languages spoken would be the official language of the new nation. English won over German by a very narrow margin.

Henry was a Saxon from Coberg, now Germany

Susan Mae Summerour was born April 14, 1859 in Walton County, Georgia, the daughter of Berry J. and Mary L. (Vineyard) Summerour. Both parents were born in Georgia.
Susan's 2nd Grandfather, Heinrich Wettin, born in Coberg, Germany on October 9, 1717, a Lutheran, died Sept. 21, 1792, and was buried in Lincoln Co., NC. The inscription on his tombstone was said to be originally written in German. His will, Dec. 7, 1790, mentions his daughter, "Elizabeth, wife of Henry Summerour."
Henry, called "Old Father Widener" in the autumn of his life, told descendants that he left Coberg over a dispute with his [half] brother, the ruler of that country, and claimed descent from Saxon rulers of Coberg [House of Wettin], disputed by some modern descendants. The Wettiner's are well known, perhaps best by Prince Albert, husband of his

first cousin Queen Victoria of England, both born much later than Heinrich. Both descend from the duke of Saxe-Coberg-Saalfield in Saxony, Germany. In records of the duke in the

Henreich Georg Witten/Whitener/Weidner, born Saxony, GR
Oct. 19, 1717
Saxony (Sachsen), Germany
Jul. 30, 1792
Lincolnton
Catawba County
North Carolina, USA

era before Heinrich's birth I found no record of descent through marriage, but the duke had 26 children out of wedlock who were recognized and supported. I think people living in that era would know their own family history. (This statement was part of a printed copy from lectures presented for the "Celebration of the Germans in North Carolina for 150 Years" and printed in the newspaper in 1894, published below). But it certainly can't be documented at this time, as far as I know. Some records today show a man considered Henry Whitener's father: I have not seen any proof for this at all. Here, his father is listed as unknown. The original inscription information for his tombstone was said to be in German-shown left. . The old one now in the churchyard is in English.

Henry was in favor of the American Revolution, a Patriot

However, his record as a supporter of the American Revolution is well documented. Some descendants have filed on this man as Henry Whitner with the NS DAR as a patriot, and the file accepted, under Ancestor number A125020, National Number 794809. In this file he is listed as Henry Whitner, NC, public service, wife Catherine Mull, she was born May 1733, PN, married at Hanover Township, Montgomery Co, PA on 26 August 1804. Henry was born 9 Oct 1717 at Coburg, Saxony, Germany, died 31 July 1792 at Lincoln Co. NC. Henry furnished supplies, source NC Rev War Pay Vouchers #4141, Tol # S.115.134.

This author has successfully applied for Patriots Henry Whitner[1] and his son-in-law Henry Summerour, who married Whitner's daughter, Elizabeth. Susan was awarded a blue ribbon on the certificate from the NS DAR as she had documented a "new patriot", Henry

---

[1] The name was difficult for those speaking English. It became , from Wettiner (one from House of Wettin, Saxony, Germany), to Wettener,"Weidner, Whitener and – in th NS DAR files - Whitner. The man is documented conclusively, but spelling was casual in Colonial times and the name difficult to spell in English.

Summerour, NC, that is one whose patriotic contribution had not been conclusively proven earlier by a direct descendent.

1741 Henry Whitener/Weidner, now 24, came to Philadelphia, Pennsylvania

By 1741 Henry, now 24, was in Philadelphia, Pennsylvania via the ship Molly, taking the Oath of Allegiance on October 17. He was known in the colonies as Wettener, Weidner, Whitner or Whitener. Not long after he arrived in America, he explored the wild country alone, beyond the Catawba River in North Carolina, trapping and hunting, accompanied at first only with his long rifle and dog. He was one of the first European's, some say the very first, to explore the area. Later, he led a colony of Germans there to settle the area near the forks in what is now Catawba County and Lincoln County, NC. A fork of the Catawba, the Henry, is named for him. Henry married Maria Katherine Muel, (Mary Mull) who became "his companion in his forest life."

Henry Summeour -- from Bavaria to Pennsylvania

Among those following him to the frontier was Henry Summerour, born Dec. 1, 1729 in Summerau, Swabia, today Bavaria. Heinrich, brother Johannes and sister Susannah left together, making their way to Rotterdam, arriving in Pennsylvania September 16, 1748, on the "Patience" under Captain John Brown. They went immediately to a German center outside Philadelphia, where all three married; within a week Heinrich Summerau married a German woman named Maria (Mary). They left soon after with a group of Saxon families following Henry Whitener to the wilderness beyond the Catawba River in North Carolina, becoming the first European settlers in a beautiful valley there.

Pioneers to the Frontier

Cherokee warriors hit the settlers, killing Abram Muel, Henry Whitener's wife's brother, and his children. His wife, Mary (born Maria Pohf) escaped only because she was driving the cattle home, saw the smoke from the fire of her home burning and hid in the cane brakes until she could go for help. She returned with some of the men, Henry Whitener among them, to find her husband and children lying dead and cold, scalped by the warriors. Only her infant, also scalped, lived on for ten days, then died at last of the wounds. The group left for South Carolina, where they stayed two years, then returned, to stay. They lived there, "carrying their lives in their hands, building their houses over springs so they would have water to drink in case of siege by the Indians, with loopholes in the rock walls from which to shoot if attacked."

The German names were "Anglicized," changed to an English version of the name.

Spelling varied, written two ways or more in the same document. Germans added "er" meaning from, from the (house of) Wettin, Wettiner; from (town of) Summerau, Summerauer, etc. Heinrich Wettiner was called Henry Weidner, and is referred to as "Old Father Weidner" in the 1894 article published in the Newton County Enterprise, which lists many versions, one Wettener. He is, without question, the same man, subject of many local histories and records.

Despite battles on the frontier, marriage between the Cherokee and new European settlers was common from Viking times forward. Cherokee tradition claims Viking blood from the era of Lief Ericson. Sequoyah, (Sikwayi), also called George Gist (1770 TN-1843 NM), was half European via his father, Nathaniel Gist, a British trader. Raised a Cherokee in Tennessee by his mother, it is said he never learned to read, write or speak English. He served with the US Army in the Creek War of 1813-14 in Alabama, in the 1830's represented his people during the Cherokee removal in Georgia, and invented the Cherokee alphabet, bringing literacy to his people. The giant Sequoia tree in California is named in his honor. Susan Summerour, 2nd great-grandchild of the folks fighting the Cherokee on the North Carolina frontier would marry a man said to be one fourth Cherokee, Porter Wininger, in Texas.

Elizabeth Whitener, daughter of Henry the Saxon, marries Henry Summerour II

Elizabeth, daughter of the Saxon leader, Henry Whitener, married Henry Summerour II in North Carolina. Land left to her by her father went to her sons, John and Henry Summerour, who sold it and moved to Walton County, Georgia, northeast of Atlanta, near the North Georgia Appalachian foothills.

Elizabeth's Grandson is a Goldminer, Strikes it Rich in California

One of Henry's sons, John Layfayette Summerour (1827-1887) born in Walton County, went with a brother to California in the Gold Rush, hit a rich vein found near Auburn, in Placer County, then returned to Dawson County, Georgia, keeping a journal of his travels. A letter home reads:

"Sluice E, American River, California,

July 20, 1851.

Dear Father,

It is with much pleasure that I this evening commence dictating a few lines to you. I received your letter of the 24 and content carefully read. It affords much satisfaction to hear from my friends from whom I am so far seperated. You have no idea how much joy it affords to us poor wonders [wanderers] to hear from home, it gives new life and stirs us up to double our energies to obtain a sufficiency to enable us to go home, home sweet home is continually ringing in our ears. I have good new to communicate. I am making money as fast as I want it. We made 7 pounds or 1680 dwts [dram weights] in one day. That was on yesterday and Thursday 1400 dwts. This whole week 8 hands made 6532 dwts 'sides shares which you will see leaves me over 1,000 dwts. Me and Bro. Frank has hands hired, we give them five dollars per diem and board them which makes about six dollars. It is a large price, but we are making a large profit on them. My individual expense is something over fifty dollars for which we have bin doing well for 6 weeks past and the profit is good as ever. I have made in that length of time 2300 dwts to myself clear of all expenses. I think by the [fort]'night week I will have 3,000. I confidently calculate on making 7000 dwts by the time I go home which I think will be a handsome sum to start home with. Perhaps you would like to know about the gold mine we have, I made the discovery myself. It is evidently the bed of some river which has for many ages past run here, but now it is many hundred feet below this spot. I believe that the north course of the American River has had its course here. If you will signal your mind to lead you to the White Path Gold Mine and mark the place on the high bluff where Chastain did so remarkable well, you will have to your view just such a mine as ours with the exception that our mine contains a heavy formation of river gravel and the gold very fine fish scales; it is so abundant we can see it in the dirt. We have panned out as much as 160 dwts at one pan. We have to run our dirt down a shoot some hundred yards, but we have surveyed a ditch 1 1/4 miles long which will bring the water on top of the hills. But we will have to wait for the rains which will be some 3 months. It thundered and rained a few drops last night, which is an uncommon thing here, it made me think of home. I have had a spell of sickness which lasted 3 weeks, I was not confined to my bed any of the time, it was cold. Bro. Frank and several has had the complaints, but we are all well now. The health of the country is very good. The Georgians are doing well so far as I know. Our company that I am connected with is Silas Worley, Tony Thornton, Frank O'Conner and Abram Whitener, we get along first rate. You must know that everybody don't agree here if they do come from the same place. There are many things that would interest you relative to this country, but I have not space to pen it sufface to say we have a great country. I must inform you that I live on the Devils Canyon, happily for us the (old man) has bin absent ever since we have bin here, may he remain so, Amen. You requested me to write you relative to some report concerning John. I can just say to you that the report is the same here. But no more than rumor can be obtained and you ought to know that all such rumors are generally two thirds lies. John has enemies in this country, heed not what you hear. Say to Alexander for me to dismiss forever from his mind the idea of coming to California. Tell him to can enjoy himself more in one day with his family than he could here in 12 months, if he could make a pound in a day. I hope I shall never meet any of my cousins here, there is plenty of gold here, but the risk is to great. Do the best you can for my littel family while I am absent and I will numerate you for your kindness when I return. I hope I am in yours and the families daily prayers, my friends as well as my enemies and daily laid before our makers throne. I need not request anymore, I will try the 15th of December to be ready to imbark for home. You must write to me upon the receipt of this. Give my love to all the family and to Joseph Seitz and family and all my friends. Bro. Frank sends his love to you and family. My love to my family through this. Bro. Frank says to Amelda to squeeze littel Frank for him. Kiss him for me. This letter must answer for you all, write me often.

Yours with affection and asteem, John L. Summerour.

Mailed to

Mr. John Spriggs

Post Master, Highfalls Post Office,

Lumpkin Co., GA

John Layfayette Summerour later put up the money to build the courthouse Adam Peck Jr. worked in as a surveyor in Lumpkin County.

John Summerour Goes to Georgia-and the Civil War Descends
His uncle, John Summerour, this writer's 2nd great-grandfather, married Margaret"Peggy" Berry in North Carolina and moved to Georgia before the birth in 1829 of his first child, Berry J. Summerour. Berry married Mary L. Vinyard in Georgia and in 1862 at age thirty-three, joined the CSA, leaving his wife Mary at home to care for his young children, Nivina, 8, Elizabeth, 7, and Susan, 3. He deserted in 1864, going home to protect his family, as many men did when invading Union forces bore down on Atlanta under General Sherman. Some of John Lafayette's family barely escaped Sherman's army, traveling for many weeks as far as Florida, then returned and stayed with "Uncle John" in Walton County until things settled down.

Margaret Berry, wife of John Summerour

The name Berry is used often to name sons by the Summerour family, a sign of great respect. Margaret (Berry) Summerour, John's mother, was born with a Scotch-Irish surname. Many in the Appalachian Mountains were Presbyterian Ulster Scots sent four generations earlier from Scotland to Ireland by the English King James I, to pacify the native Catholic Celts in Ireland, who built in north Ireland the same log cabins and "pales" (fences, sometimes in the form of vertical log barricades creating a fort, sometimes split rail fences) later found in America.

Log cabins, Germanic in origin, were found on the European continent, in England and Scotland. Examples of one type was found in a Saxon Church built in Essex, England in 1013. They spread throughout Scandinavia, North Ireland and the American Frontier. Those who became in north Ireland the Scotch-Irish or Ulster Scots were primarily Lowland Scots. Many of them found English laws passed repressing religious freedom and increases in rent after their 99 year leases expired unbearable, migrating in great numbers to the American Colonies, where they inter-married with the Germans in North Carolina. Afterward, their bitterness toward the English was so great that George Washington said he could not have prevailed in the revolution without "the Scotch-Irish, who rode at once to fight with gun and horse while the English and the Germans [in America] pondered what to do."

The Scots in the Lowlands were primarily Anglo-Saxon's from the north of England, who invaded Scotland after the Norman conquest in 1066 and pushed the Celtic Scots into the highlands. William Wallace, a knight's son called "Braveheart," was a lowland Scot who waged war against English rule in early Scotland and was executed in London in 1305. The Anglo-Saxons were the same who left northern Germany in the 7th century, one branch northward to invade England; another south to claim Thuringia and much of what is now Bavaria, but then Saxony, founding the dukedom of Saxe-Coberg-Saalfield. These Saxons were adventuresome folks!

....

The Summerour Brothers in the Civil War*

By Susan Moore Teller, July 17, 2014 [1]

The brothers John Summerour Jr. and Berry Summerour are both shown as enlisted in the CSA 42nd Regiment GA Militia; both muster in on the 4th of March 1862 in Walton Co GA. The original hand written muster document is on file, showing the name of both men.

Later, Berry Summerour of Social Circle, Walton Co, Georgia is shown in extensive original document records (33 pages) in the Federal Archives as a Private in Company D, 2nd Regiment, Georgia Calvary, CSA enlisted on May 1, 1862 for the duration of the war. His CSA document states he traveled 77 miles to enlist. It looks like they may have both enlisted first in the 42nd Regiment, GA Militia, as we have copies of the original documents showing both men in the muster for Walton County, Georgia; then later Berry enlists in a different company. We found no further CSA military record of John Summerour Jr. He is on record in the Walton County Tax Digest as: B.(…erry…) Summerour, administrator for the estate of John Summerour Jr. Berry is shown as the executor for his father, John Summerour Sr. in the same document, both died 1863 Walton County, Georgia.

Since Berry is shown as the executor (of John Sr.) administrator (for John Jr.)of his deceased brother and father's estates in 1863, apparently John Jr. was wounded, and died of his wounds sometime later as his brother Berry is named administrator of John Jr.'s estate and John Jr's children by Nancy Vineyard, his first wife, are some are assigned to guardians Berry and Mary (…Vineyard…) Summerour in the Walton County Georgia Probate Records. In the US CN of GA in1870: James Berry Summerour b 1853 age 18 is living in the George family household, as is his younger brother, George. In another GA household the widow Mary Summerour, i.e. Mary Carter, second wife of John Summerour Jr. is living with her two young daughters, the younger born October 1863. In short, the family history that states they raised these boys as their own and educated John Jr. and Nancy's three sons, James Berry Summerour, William Franklin Summerour and George Stephen Summerour is partially true. However, in 1876 Berry Summerour asks the court to be relieved of guardianship of brother John Summerour's estate: note John's son James Berry Summerour, born 1853 is now of age. James Berry Summerour born 1853 remains in Georgia and lives and dies there, as does his younger brother, George. Some of their direct descendants live in Georgia today. Berry's son, also named James Berry Summerour, born 1864 goes with his parents and siblings to Texas, and direct descendants live in Texas today. Family members have said the Berry Summerour family left for Texas and returned only once: at the death of Margaret "Peggy" Berry, wife of John Summerour Sr. Berry is again named executor of her estate.

John Summerour Jr. is said in family histories to have died of wounds received in the Civil War. His brother Berry is named administrator of his brother John Summerour Jr. AND John Summerour Sr.'s estate in 1863 Walton County Georgia Probate Records; Berry and Mary (…Vineyard…) Summerour are named guardians and Berry the administrator of John Summerour Jr.'s estate, thus his death date may be 1863.

Berry is also wounded later and so listed in 1862 CSA records in the Federal Archives, but recovers, unlike his brother who died of wounds received in the civil war.

Berry Summerour of Social Circle, Walton Co GA is listed as AWOL three separate times:

a) the first from a hospital in Dalton Co GA in late 1862 after a three months stay due to "Icterus" [2] --. After recovering from the Jaundice caused by Hepatitis A, he returned to duty, and is so recorded. He did leave the hospital without an official discharge after 3 months and is listed as AWOL as a result.

b) Berry (Pvt. Company D, 2nd Georgia Calvary, Capt. Moore) is listed as absent in November and December of 1863 because he is wounded. This is the same date time frame that he appears in Walton County Georgia Probate Court and is appointed administrator of both John Summerour Sr.'s estate and John Summerour Jr.'s estate in 1863. Clearly, both brothers were wounded; however, John Jr. later dies of his injuries. Berry continues on to lead the family as "executor and administrator" of both his father and his brother's estates. John Jr's first wife, Nancy Vinyard died in childbirth in 1857. His second wife, Mary Carter, continues to care for her daughters by John Jr. John's orphaned sons by Nancy are put in the guardianship of Berry and Mary Vinyard Summerour, siblings of the deceased. These papers document John Jr's death as occurring in 1863, while his memorial tombstone reads 1865. I have found no source doc for this date, so am using the documented 1863: where his brother is administrator of John Jr.'s estate.

c) Berry's third and final AWOL comes on November 1, 1864. He said he went home to Social Circle, Walton County, Georgia, after the death of his brother, and the invasion of

Sherman into Georgia, to protect his wife Mary, and –our family was told - the children of both his dead brother and sister-in-law John Summerour Jr. and Nancy Vinyard. They are so listed in GA court records, as guardians. Yet the 1870 census shows James Berry Summerour b 1853, age 18 and his brother George in the Georgia home of the George family. John Jr.'s second wife, Mary Carter, is living in another Georgia household with her two daughters by John.

By 1876, Berry asks the court to be removed as the administrator of the estate of his brother. (John Jr.'s oldest son, James Berry Summerour is now 22). By 1880, the Berry and Mary Vineyard Summerour family, including their son James Berry Summerour born 1864, namesake of the older man, in living in Grayson Co TX. Their granddaughter, Lela Elizabeth Wininger, daughter of their daughter Susan Mae, told this author in person her folks went by covered wagon to Texas.

Berry's third and final AWOL, then, comes on November 1, 1864. He told family descendants he went home, after the death of his brother, and the invasion of Sherman into Georgia, to protect his wife Mary L "Polly", and the children of both his dead brother and sister-in-law John Summerour Jr. and Nancy Vinyard. The children were:
1) James Berry Summerour, born 1852, now twelve,
2) William Franklin Summerour, born 1855 and about nine, and
3) George Stephen Summerour, born 1857 and about seven,
    and Berry's own children by his wife Mary Vineyard,
4) Mary Levina Summerour, born in 1854, now ten;
5) Elizabeth Summerour, born in 1855, now about nine, and
6) Susan Mae Summerour, born 14 April 1859, and now five. Susan Mae is this author's ancestor.

Mary Vinyard Summerour was living in Social Circle, Walton County, Georgia on November 1, 1864, feeding and caring for several children between five and twelve, with Sherman's Army on the march through Georgia. Berry went home to aid her. Social Circle is about five miles from the main road to Augusta, the destination of the left wing of Sherman's Army. She was alone. Berry went AWOL to protect her and the children.

Sherman's March to the Sea is the name commonly given to the military Savannah Campaign in the American Civil War, conducted through Georgia from November 1 to December 21, 1864 by Major Gen. William Tecumseh Sherman of the Union Army. The campaign began with Sherman's troops leaving the captured city of Atlanta, Georgia, on November 15 and ended with the capture of the port of Savannah on December 21. His forces destroyed military targets as well as industry, infrastructure, and civilian property and disrupted the South's economy and its transportation networks. Sherman's bold move of operating deep within enemy territory and without supply lines is considered to be revolutionary in the annals of war.[3] However, this did mean the soldiers survived by "foraging" or confiscating food from local residents as the army advanced. This made life very hazardous for the women and children at home alone.

A book, the novel, *Cracker Cavaliers: The 2nd Georgia Cavalry Under Wheeler and Forrest* – October 1, 2000 by John Randolph Poole is the story of the 2nd Georgia Calvary. This is the regiment Berry Summerour was in throughout the civil war, following a few months with his brother and brother-in-law in the 41st Reg. of GA from Walton County, GA. A preview reads: *Cracker Cavaliers: The 2nd Georgia Cavalry under Wheeler and Forrest documents the regiment's participation in major campaigns of the western theater, including the Atlanta Campaign and Sherman's March to the Sea from an ordinary soldier's perspective on the Civil War. (Definition of a "cracker" - those who cracked their whips over the oxen pulling their wagons westward, i.e. derogatory term for wagon train pioneers. A "cavalier" is a person with noble blood. Many "second sons" from noble families came to colonial America to make their own fortune as they would not inherit due to primogenture, i.e. oldest son gets everything. Others were from families "out of favor" with the current ruler, and in danger of persecution in England. Some folks were even beheaded, hung or burned at the stake).*

From the first conflict under General Nathan Bedford Forrest at Murfreesboro in 1862 to the desperate and often brutal battles with Union cavalry in the Carolinas during 1865, the Second Georgia was almost constantly in action. While the Second Georgia fought in such famous campaigns as Perryville, Stones River, Chickamauga, Knoxville, Resaca, Atlanta, and Bentonville, they also participated in deadly encounters at Farmington, Mossy Creek, Noonday Creek, Sunshine Church, and Waynesboro. Many of these conflicts are obscure to all but the most ardent Civil War historians. This is the first regimental history of a Georgia Cavalry regiment ever published. The Second Georgia served under both Nathan Bedford Forrest and Joe Wheeler, and campaigned not only on home turf, but literally on the farm acreages of many of the unit's members. This is the company Berry Summerour was in from March of 1862 through November 1 of 1864.

Both President Lincoln and General Ulysses S. Grant had serious reservations about Sherman's plans.[5] Still, Grant trusted Sherman's assessment and on November 2, 1864, he sent Sherman a telegram stating simply, "Go as you propose."[6] The 300-mile (480 km) march began on November 15. Sherman recounted in his memoirs the scene when he left at 7 a.m. the following day:

..."*We rode out of Atlanta by the Decatur road, filled by the marching troops and wagons of the Fourteenth Corps; and reaching the hill, just outside of the old rebel works, we naturally paused to look back upon the scenes of our past battles. We stood upon the very ground whereon was fought the bloody battle of July 22d, and could see the copse of wood where McPherson fell. Behind us lay Atlanta, smoldering and in ruins, the black smoke rising high in air, and hanging like a pall over the ruined city. Away off in the distance, on the McDonough road, was the rear of Howard's column, the gun-barrels glistening in the sun, the white-topped wagons stretching away to the south; and right before us the Fourteenth Corps, marching steadily and rapidly, with a cheery look and swinging pace, that made light of the thousand miles that lay between us and Richmond. Some band, by accident, struck up the anthem of "John Brown's soul goes marching on;" the men caught up the strain, and never before or since have I heard the chorus of "Glory, glory, hallelujah!" done with more spirit, or in better harmony of time and place."*

— William T. Sherman , *Memoirs of General W.T. Sherman, Chapter 21*

42nd Regiment, Georgia Infantry (Confederate) Source: *United States   U.S. Military   Georgia   Georgia Military   Georgia in the Civil War   42nd Regiment, Georgia Infantry (Confederate)*

Contents [1 Brief History](#)
- [2 Companies in this Regiment with the Counties of Origin](#)
- [3 Other Sources](#)
- 4 References

Brief History This regiment was assembled at Camp McDonald, Georgia, in March, 1862, with men from Gwinnett, De Kalb, Newton, Walton, Fulton, and Calhoun counties. National Park Service, [1]

Companies in this Regiment with the Counties of Origin Men often enlisted in a company recruited in the counties where they lived though not always. After many battles, companies might be combined because so many men were killed or wounded. However if you are unsure which company your ancestor was in, try the company recruited in his county first.

Members of this regiment were enlisted from the following Georgia counties: Gwinnett, De Kalb, Newton, Walton, Fulton, and Calhoun counties.[2]

↑ Calhoun, William Lowndes. *History of the 42nd Regiment, Georgia Volunteers, Confederate States Army, Infantry*. (Atlanta, Georgia: s.n., 1900). FHL 975.8 A1 no.63
Source- Retrieved from
"https://familysearch.org/learn/wiki/en/42nd_Regiment,_Georgia_Infantry_(Confederate)"

Category: Georgia - Military - Civil War, 1861-1865

[1] *(copyright by Susan Moore Teller, July 17, 2014, Peoria AZ)*

[2] Icterus: i.e. jaundice- can be caused by Hepatitis A: Hepatitis A is a type of liver inflammation that occurs due to the hepatitis A virus. This short-term infection often resolves within a few months. Symptoms include yellow eyes and skin. Hepatitis is an inflammation of the liver caused by exposure to toxins, immune diseases, or infection. Viruses cause most cases of hepatitis. Hepatitis A is an acute (short-term) type of hepatitis, which usually requires no treatment. According to the World Health Organization, 1.4 million cases of hepatitis A occur each year. This highly contagious form of hepatitis can cause epidemics through contaminated food or water. Luckily, it is not serious, and usually causes no long-term effects. Certain factors can increase risk of contracting it, including living in (or spending an extended time in) an area where hepatitis A is common—this includes most developing countries, or primitive living conditions. Note Berry left the CSA Hospital in Dalton, GA (i.e. was AWOL, i.e.was absent without leave) after three months. It seems he went home, and recovered, as he later returned to duty. Berry lived to be an old man.
[3] Source: Wikipedia

....

The Summerour Pioneer Westward to Texas, and the Wininger Connection

John and Margaret (Berry) Summerour left Georgia after 1873 with children Susan Mae, James Berry, William D., and George W., settling in the famous "Red River Valley" before 1880. Lela, Susan's daughter, often told grandchildren that her folks came to Texas in a covered wagon. The journey from Walton County was about 800 miles, at five miles a day, the trip must have taken over five months. In 1880, we find Susan, 21, in Greyson County, Texas with her parents, Mary L., 47, Berry J. Summerour, 52; siblings James B., 15, William D., 12, and George W., 7, all born in Georgia. Later, a descendant, Delvin Black, found a marriage certificate for Porter Kalvin Wininger and "Susie Johnigan" – we know this woman is the 25 year old Susan Mae Summerour, who must have had a first husband and is now a young widow at her second marriage. By 1900, Susan, now 41, is living in nearby Montague Co., TX, with her husband of fifteen years, Porter Wininger, 45, born in Tennessee (Porter's father Levi said he was born in Illinois, and I think the census taker must have asked him where he was "from". The Wininger's were "from" Hawkins Co., Tennessee, where P.K. was actually born, but lived in Illinois later) and children Cora, 12, Lela, 10; Angeline, 9; Clemmie, 7; Osker, 4; Willie, 2; and Athel, six months, all born in Texas. Porter was a widower at their marriage. Porter married first, Julia Howeth, in Cooke Co., Texas, July 6, 1876. Julia died, leaving 3 children, Alvin, Dora and Virgie who lived with kinfolk. His second wife was twenty-five year old Susan (Summerour) Johnigan, and Porter her second husband. Susan died in 1926. He married two times afterward, a total of four times according to granddaughter Myrl (Moore) Ward and died again a widower at 96, in Troup, Smith Co., Texas. He was buried at Brushy Cemetery in Bowie, Texas.

Levi Wininger, Porter Kalvin Wininger's father, descends from Clementz Dunkelberger and Nicholaus Weininger, who came to America in the ship Priscilla, arriving 12 September, 1750, to the port of Philadelphia. Nicholaus Weininger's son, Andrew, married Clemens Dunkelberger's daughter, Catharina, and is listed in Dunkelberger's will, written 12 Feb. 1776, which states: "Secondly, my will is that my son-in-law, Andrew Wininger and his wife Catharina shall make no demand against my executors for I have given them their full share." Catherine and Andrew Wininger went to Scott, Co. VA, bordering Hawkins County, TN (near Kingsport) in the Appalachian Mountains.

Levi Wininger, who is my 2nd great-grandfather, was born in Hawkins Co., East TN, the second son of a large family. The German language was still used (in this country) and Levi spoke English with a heavy brogue, pronouncing his "W's" like "V's". He always called his son William, "Villiam". He left Tennessee to go west at about eight years of age, with his father Adam, his mother, Mary M. (*Some descendants state her middle name was Magdelene, some say Margaret), his brother and sisters settling in Jackson Co. IN in 1831.

They traveled along the Wilderness Road, to the Vincennes Trace in Indiana, to Jackson County. Levi's father is Adam, and my conclusion, after viewing conflicting family histories by different descendants, is that his grandfather is probably Phillip, whose will refers to son Adam, but some families say Adam Wininger is William Wininger's son. All lines by different families go back to the same Nicholas Wininger, tracing the family from Germany to Pennsylvania, to Hawkins Co., TN, then the central Indiana Counties, then Salem Co., Illinois, on still further west by wagon train to north Texas, and then some winding back up from Texas to Southwest Indian Territory and western Arkansas near the Oklahoma border.

Levi had moved on to Salem, Marion Co., IL by the time the 1850 census and is shown, which I viewed on film of original census, with wife Nancy and their children born by 1850).

Levi Wininger left Jackson Co. IN for Salem. Marion County, IL upon reaching the age to marry, to make his own way. At the age of twenty, he married sixteen year old Nancy Ann Powell, the daughter of William Powell and his wife, Nancy Porter.

Levi and Nancy had seven children, all born in Salem, Marion Co. IL; William Powell, James Narton, Elizabeth Ann, Jacob, Mary Catherine, Porter Kalvin and John M. Nancy died at the birth of her 7th child, John M. Wininger., in 1857, "in the first part of the year, before she was 31 years old."

Porter Kalvin, my great-grandfather, was just under two years of age when his mother died in the early part of the year before her 31st birthday in the year 1857 in Jackson Co., IN. His father, Levi, married again within the year to another "full blooded" German girl, Arabella Gillian, who was about the same age as Levi's oldest son, William Powell, by Nancy, his first wife. (Census data consistently over 3 decades says she was born in 1840, thus age 17 upon her marriage in 1857. Still close to William Powell's age, but 3 years older, not same age).

Arabella, according to the book "The Genealogy of the Wininger Family in America" by Mercedes Bowen, was "very heavyset, and not much loved by her step-children." Her eldest stepson, William Powell Wininger did not get along with her at all, and left for Texas, 1500 miles away, when he was not quite 14, on foot. He settled in Gainsville, Cook Co. TX and sent for his two young brothers, Porter Kalvin and James M. within a year. By 1860, Levi had sold all his land in Indiana (see Land Records) and moved with his second wife, Arabella and the remaining children by Nancy, to Cook Co. TX, where he is found July 7, 1860 with 2nd wife shown as Anabel, age 20 (this is Arabella Gillian) keeping house, and children William, 17; Jim, 11; Elizabeth, 10; Jacob, 8; Porter, 5; John, 3; and Andrew J. two months, (later renamed Vincent T.) the only child on the census born in Texas, rather than in Illinois, the two month old son, by Arabella, who lost one child shortly after birth in IL, named Andrew J. This is the boy they later renamed Vinson or Vincent. Mary Catherine, Nancy's child born two years before Porter Kalvin, has apparently died before 1860, as she is not shown with the family.

While Porter Kalvin Wininger, according to MMWB's grandfather, joined his brother William Powell Wininger as a young boy, after his father and stepmother moved to Sebastian Co. AR he moved with them, as he is living with them at age 16.

The 1870 Sebastian Co. AR Federal Census shows, in Sugarloaf Township, house # 40, Wininger, L. 48, WM Farmer, (given name very hard to read, but does look like census taker wrote "Luther" instead of Levi in error), with Rebella, 30, WF, keeping house, (this is Arabelle/Arabella Gillian, Levi's his 2nd wife), Jacob, 19 WM, at home, Porter, 16, WM, at home (this is Porter Kalvin Wininger, SMT's Great Grandfather), John, 13, WM, at home, Vinson, 11, WM, at home, (this child was called Andrew Jackson, same name as the earlier born brother who died, in the 1860 Cook Co., TX census, by the time of this census Levi and Arabella had changed the child's name to Vinson or Vincent, which is on his tombstone in Hartford, AR); Benjamin, 6, WM, at home, Mary, 5, WF, at home, and Nicholas, 2 WM, at home.

Levi, 38 years old at the start of the Civil War, left Gainsville, (known for its confederate sympathies -- which included some hangings of those unsympathetic to the southern cause) -- because he had northern sympathies. Three of Levi's brothers, Kalvin S., James, and Wesley, were in the USA Army, whom he feared he might be forced to shoot if he were impressed in the CSA. Levi had a son, William P., who joined the CSA Army while still 17, whom he feared might be forced to shoot if he were impressed in the USA forces. He wished to avoid serving in either army for this reason. He left Texas sometime after July of 1860, and moved to Hartford, AR, homesteading land filed on the date of May 20, 1862. Levi lived on Prairie Creek, about five miles north of Hartford, about a miles from Midland and 23 miles southwest of Fort Smith, in the Sugar Loaf Mountain area. He lived in a large log cabin he built that sat near a large cliff of rocks that formed a cave, near the foot of Sugar Loaf Mountain in a narrow valley about five miles across. It was an isolated valley, near caves where he hid in when soldiers from either side came near, fed by his wife Arabella until they were gone.

His brother James, 35 years of age at enlistment in Medora IN, mustered in 31 Dec. 1863 at Camp Horton, KY, was 6 ft. 1 inch, black hair, black eyes, dark complexion, was taken prisoner in Terre Noir, Arkansas on April 2, 1864, and died at the hands of the enemy in Tyler TX. Levi's brother Kalvin, age 38 at enlistment in Medora, IL, as a corporal in the USA Army, mustered in at Camp Horton, KY, was wounded in action on Dec. 31, 1862, left in General Hospital in Jackson, TN was never afterward well, and received a govt. pension for his service. Levi's brother Wesley was killed March 24, 1864 while serving with USA forces in Richmond. Levi's son, William Powell Wininger enlisted at seventeen from Gainesville TX in the CSA as a private and served as a scout and courier for four years in this capacity for Robert E. Lee, at times carrying messages between Robert E. Lee and USA General U. L. Grant, whom he also came to know well. William Powell Wininger was with the same group still guarding General Robert E. Lee at the time of his surrender. to US forces. William was captured for a time, but was either released or escaped, as he made his way home after the war.

Levi did not wish to join in this fight, and hid his person as well as food and supplies in caves near his home in Hartford until the war was over, as he greatly feared killing a son or brother in that conflict. Levi lived in Arkansas until his death in 1898, and his tombstone can be found in Lot 117, Harford Cemetery, Sebastian County, AR. However, his descendants put up the tombstone in the 1940's and knew his death date, but did not know his correct birthdate, which is grossly in error.

Levi was born in Hawkins Co., TN, moved as a child to Indiana with his parents, went as a young man to Salem Co., IL, where he married Nancy Ann, then moved to Texas with Arabella where one child was born, then on to Sebastian Co., AR where the remainder of their children were born and they both are buried. Nancy Ann died in Salem Co., Illinois. Most of his children by Nancy Ann remained in Cook Co., TX or nearby.

Levi left Texas as the Civil War began, moving to a secluded area of Sebastian Co., Arkansas near Sugar Loaf Mountain, hiding in nearby caves when the soldiers came around to take men. He had brothers still in Indiana fighting on the northern side, a son in the CSA, and was terrified he might be forced to kill a family member if he were to go in either army. Arabella would bring him food at night till all the military men left the area.

His oldest son, William Powell Wininger joined the CSA, served as a scout and guard for General Robert E. Lee, and was one of the special guards with General Robert E. Lee at his surrender in Richmond, VA. William Powell had a large family, and lived in Cook Co. TX many years. He went to Texas as a boy of not quite 14, because he didn't get along with his new stepmother, only 3 years his senior. William Powell sent for his two youngest brothers, Jacob and Porter as soon as he could, and later his father Levi followed with Arabella and the rest of the children, but didn't stay long, going on to Sebastian Co., AR. Porter Kalvin Wininger, age 16, is found in Sebastian Co. AR with his father and stepmother, but is back in

Cook Co. Texas upon his first marriage to Julia Howeth, sister to William Powell's wife, Cynthia Ann Howeth, both daughters of John Howeth and Urethra Melissa Ann (Doyle) Howeth. Porter married 2nd, Susan Mae (Summerour) Johnigan, my great-grandmother, who also had a first marriage behind her.

There are Summerour and Wininger descendants in Texas and Oklahoma along the Red River basin region down to this era.

These people were not the very first to come to Texas or Oklahoma, but they were pioneers who came in covered wagons and lived the life of the pioneer, building their own log cabins, making their own soap, raising their own food, and living with well water and outhouses, cellars put in for protection from storms and to hold a good food supply for bad years, making their own way with no help from anyone but their own folks in hard times. They deserve to be remembered by their descendants.

Hickory, North Carolina June 13, 1894 –
The History of the Saxons To North Carolina Published in 1894

The article below was published in the Newton Enterprise, Hickory, NC, 1894:

Hickory, North Carolina - June 13, 1894
Introduction by J.L. Murphy (printed in local newspaper, The Newton Enterprise following Henry Weidner Memorial Service)

On the first Sunday in April, 1894, at Bethel Reformed Church, Mr. John W. Robinson asked the pastor's permission to make a few remarks after the service. He stated that near his home, on the hill, rested the ashes of Henry Weidner, the first white settler of the south fork Valley. The grave was said to be covered with briars, and the fence surrounding it in a dilapidated condition. Mr. Robinson appealed to the friends to rebuild the fence, and to beautify the grave, adding that it was his desire that a suitable service be held at some convenient time.

This was the first intimation of the Henry Weidner Memorial Service. This writer was asked to prepare a program for the occasion, which he did, selecting the 30th day of May as the time. Being properly advertised and suitable provisions being made, the largest crowd assembled on that day that has ever been brought together at one time, within the history of this community, being between 2,500 and 3,000 people present.

The interest manifested by this audience was intense. The speakers had made careful and extended preparations; the choirs had selected the most soul stirring music. After the service was over, a general request came up from the friends asking that the proceedings of the day should be published in pamphlet form. Yielding to that request, we have gathered together the speeches made and the papers read on that day, and herewith give them to the public, trusting that they will inspire reverence in the hearts of the young for their parents, and awaken an interest in someone who will write more fully than before about the history of the German people who settled this part of western North Carolina. To Judge McCorkle and Colonel G. M. Yoder, we are indebted for their invaluable papers. We give the program as rendered that day without embellishment, or comment.

Another: ARTICLE PUBLISHED IN THE NEWSPAPER "The Newton Enterprise"

Catawba County, North Carolina, May, 1894

Report of the exercises held at the old pioneer's homestead in Catawba County, North Carolina, May 3Oth, 1894. The gathering at the home of Mr. Robinson is told in this manner, by the Newton Enterprise

Wednesday morning, May 3Oth dawned upon us dark and gloomy, the heavy clouds hung low, and threatened each moment to deluge the earth with rain, but nothing daunted, large numbers of persons were easily to be seen wending their way to the hospitable home of Mr. John W. Robinson, to attend the memorial services to be held that day in honor of Henry Weidner, the discoverer of South Fork, and earliest settler of that part of Catawba County.

Mr. Robinson's Address

On nearing the home of our friend, Mr. Robinson was to be seen standing in his front yard bidding a hearty welcome to each and every visitor as they passed by him, be they in buggy, carriage, wagon, cart, on horseback, or on foot. When we reached the grounds, it looked as if hundreds had preceded us and still long lines of vehicles could be seen as far down the road as the eye could reach. A nice platform had been erected beneath the out-stretching branches of that giant oak tree, which has borne upon its bark the red paint, that was the Indian's signal to Henry Weidner and his noble comrades that hostilities had commenced, and the trunk of this mighty white oak as well as the speakers platform had been prettily decorated for the occasion.

At 10:30 the chorus of Bethel and Zion gave the audience some very appropriate music and Rev. Mr. Murphy, who was master of ceremonies, announced the invocation by Rev. A. H. Smith, following with the scripture lessons, Genesis 17: 1-8; Hebrew 11:322-40, by Rev. Mr. Murphy, and prayer by the Rev. Prof. Cline of Lenoir College. Following the prayer, the choirs sang All Hail The Power of Jesus Name." Mr. John W. Robinson was then introduced, who delivered the address of welcome.

John W. Robinson's Address:

Mr. Robinson spoke as follows: Ladies and Gentlemen: I am truly thankful that I have been permitted to see this day on which the descendants and friends of Henry Weidner have assembled under this old historic tree, which stands as a living monument to his memory, to do the honor to the old pioneer of the south Fork Valley. Nearby, now in ruins, is the home, and on yonder hill is the last resting place of the first white man who saw the beautiful valley of Henry's and Jacob's Forks of South Fork of the Catawba River.

And now to you, the living relatives of Old Father Weidner, to you kind pastors and your people, to you neighbors and friends, to all, I, in behalf of my family and self, extend a most cordial welcome to my home - - once the home of Father Weidner.

Young ladies and young men, little boys and girls, please hear me: I am thankful to you for being here today with us, as living, blooming, budding flowers, to help decorate this memorial service to the honor of our dear old father and mother. In behalf of my wife, my sons, and my daughters, I extend to you a heartfelt welcome.

Now shall we remember the relatives in other States? I can say, if they were here, with out-stretched arms, we would greet them and say; "Welcome, welcome once more to the old homestead, and the last resting place of our father and mother. Great-grand children, please give me your attention. This memorial service was mostly gotten up for your benefit. I congratulate you on having such a brave and great man as Henry Weidner for your ancestor. I trust you will pay good attention to the speakers who we have with us today. We are on the down grade. Soon our race will be run, and what history may be handed down to you today, I trust you will keep in your minds so you may be able to tell your children and grandchildren. I extend to you a loving welcome. I take occasion, also to express my thanks to the kind friends who have so nobly assisted in fencing the old family graveyard, and in beautifying the grave of Father Weidner. To the committee of arrangement, to the choirs of Zion and Bethel churches, I return my sincere thanks. In conclusion I appeal to all for good order."

Rev. Murphy's Address:

At the conclusion of Mr. Robinson's address, Rev. Mr. Murphy arose and said:

"Mr. Robinson, in behalf of this large assemblage of people, the descendants and friends of Henry Weidner, I sincerely thank you for the lively interest you have manifested in this memorial service. You conceived the thought of holding this service, you planned it, you have given time and energy to it, you have thrown open the doors of your home, you have given us a warm welcome. I thank you for the opportunity of learning something of our ancestry, and for the privilege of honoring the brave man who first discovered and settled this beautiful valley of the South Fork of the Catawba.

There is no better way of impressing the important lessons of life upon the minds of our young people than by pointing them to the noble deeds of these ancestors.

A certain Latin writer has said that whenever he beheld the images of his ancestors, he felt his mind vehemently excited to virtue. It was not the wax of marble that possessed and inspired this power, but the recollections of their noble actions, which kindled this generous flame in his bosom. The learned apostle, when he would arouse the Hebrew Christians and inspire then to noble deeds and to greater and truer reverence, rehearsed the lives of the heroes of faith who subdued kingdoms and wrought righteousness. We feel that today will gather fresh inspiration which will enable us to go on to higher attainments and greater perfection in life. Again, we sincerely thank you.""

Rev. J. C. Clapp, D.D.; president of Catawba College, was then introduced as the orator selected to deliver the memorial sermon. Dr. Clapp was followed by the Rev. J.C. Moser, pastor of the Holy Trinity Lutheran Church, of Hickory, North Carolina, in an appropriate address. The addresses of Dr. Clapp and Rev. Moser were delivered without notes, and we are unable to give them.

At this point, a recess of one hour and a half was taken. The large audience was invited to visit the grave of Henry Weidner and the hill nearby, which most of them did. Returning from the grave, the audience was invited to surround the large table arranged in the field above the Robinson's house.

After a few words of prayer by the Rev. Prof. R. A. Yoder, President of Lenoir College, the invitation was given to partake of the dinner with which the large table was loaded. After dinner some time was spent on social chat when the crowd reassembled around the stand, and

Judge Matthew L. McCorkle, of Newton, was introduced and spoke as follows:

Colonel McCorkle's Speech

Ladies and Gentlemen:

It has been customary among all civilized people since the world was created, to build monuments to perpetuate the memories of the noble dead, and celebrate great events in the world's history.

Sometimes hundreds of years elapse, before the deeds of the distinguished dead are appreciated. Columbus, the discoverer of America, never received the honors that were due him until the celebration of the 4OOth anniversary of the discovery of America. Washington, the great father of his country, was never honored before, as he was on the celebration of the completion of the monument, 515 feet high, in Washington City.

It has been over one hundred and fifty years since Henry Weidner first discovered yonder beautiful river, the South Fork of the Catawba River.

When he (..Henry Weidner/ Wettner /Whitener..) came here, …. there were no Europeans living in the region… When Henry Weidner crossed the Catawba river at Sherrill's Fork, he was in the country of the Catawba Indians. They inhabited along the great river from near the South Carolina line to its head including all its tributaries. The home of the grant Catawba is an Indian name, and means catfish river. From Adam Sherrill's, about the year 1745, he started west without a human soul to pilot him or to accompany him in this unknown land, inhabited by nature's wild beasts and probably hostile Indians. He was armed with a gun whose barrel was about six feet long, with a tomahawk, and a long knife in his scabbard. The country away from the water courses was made of timber. He could see for miles around him and before him. With a compass, he could steer a straight direction.

Due west from Sherrill's Fork carried him to where the two rivers of the south Fork came together. He stood upon the hill not far from Ilkannah Hunsucker's and viewed the landscape o'er. Moses himself was not more delighted to view the Land of Canaan.

On his way from Sherrill's Fork to this delightful spot, he frequently saw heads of deer scampering over the plain, large flocks of wild turkeys and groves of buffalo feeding at a distance, and the wolf and coyote bounding along before him. The country was full of wild game. The earth was covered with luscious grapes and nourishing pea vines. The streams abounded in fish of all kinds. There were no dams and nets and wire seines stretched across the river to obstruct the fish from coming from the ocean and the steams were not filled with sand in consequence of bad farming. Nature was herself untarnished. The two forks united about a half a mile further up Jacob's Fork than they do now. The low ground was covered with tall cane, with here and there a large walnut on the banks or otherwise. It is said he crossed the on a raft over the river and he thought there was but one stream. He found its mate. Which one if the larger, no one knows to this day. Signs of otter, mink, musk rat, coon, and bear could be seen all along the banks of either stream, or behold the soil as fertile as the valley of the river Nile. Henry Weidner might have exclaimed, Gefunden! then raised his eyes to heaven and thanked God, for his goodness and mercies endureth forever. Night overtook him; he laid himself down to sleep with his watch dogs beside him and his Heavenly Father to guard him from the dangers of the night. One of these beautiful rivers is named Henry, and the other Jacob, after Henry and Jacob Weidner.

Henry Weidner was a bold and daring adventurer. He came originally from Germany. His name passed through different forms of spelling; first (..Wettin, in German, Wetting...) W-E-T-N-E-R, then W-E-I-D-N-E-R, W-I-T-E-N-E-R, then finally W-H-II-T-E-N-E-R. (,,,Note: Germans might say they are from Berlin, or "Berliners", or if from [the house of] Wettin, "Wettiners"; Albert is from the House of Wettin, Coberg branch. If Henry's story is accurate, he was a member of the House of Wettin, a famous German dynasty. Male's in this dynasty frequently produced children outside marriage, as marriages were often very politically motivated. Such offspring were recognized and often provided for very well. We should keep in mind that Henry may have been the product of such a liaison..)

Henry The Saxon Pioneers North Carolina

He was a Saxon, from Coburg, Saxony, and left that country when he was a young man, on account of some trouble between him and his brothers about the Crown of that government, and came to America."

He landed first in Philadelphia, then came to North Carolina. Henry Weidner was kin to the family of Prince Albert's father, whose original name was Wetner. the first white man to discover the beautiful South Fork of the great Catawba. He lived in peace with the Indians, who still held the soil."

(...Editors note: it was in fact Wettin. Price Albert's family was called the House of Wettin, which was changed to Windsor by English Royal Decree in 1917 so it would sound less German. In recent encyclopedias it is referred to as the House of Saxe-Coberg instead of Wettin, as in older reference books. If our Henry was part of this family, it seems it was an unrecorded birth, probably a product of one of the many mistresses of the male ruling members of this royal family which produced 26 children.)

He was want to go back to the civilized world each spring and carry his pelts on pack horses. Some of the patents of his land bear date in 1750. on one of his trips, he brought his companion of his forest life a young wife, Catherine Mull and a youth by the name of Conrad Yoder, the ancestor of a large and respectable posterity. He also brought with him Abram Mull who had married Mary Poff. These families had not been long in their forest homes, till a band of marauding Cherokees from beyond the mountains invaded their new homes and killed Abraham Mull and two of his children, and scalped them and burned their home. Mrs. Mull had gone out to drive up the cattle and approaching near the house, the cattle came running back and that alarmed her..

She saw the smoking ruins of her home. She ran to Henry Weidner's and gave the warning and they all fled to the cane brake, and stayed there all night. The next morning Henry Weidner came back, and saw the smoldering ruins and Abram Mull lying cold and dead. The children had been killed and all of their scalps taken off. Oh, what a heart rendering scene to the poor bereaved wife and mother and all who beheld it! They were ready to exclaim, "Carry me back, carry me back to old Sylvania's shore. " The Indians had killed some of their cattle and had gone. Henry Weidner and family and Mrs. Mull went to South Carolina, and after they had been there a short time, Henry Weidner and John Warlick came back to reconnoiter the country. They saw a band of Indians not far from the old homestead. They retreated and Warlick's horse became mired and while he was trying to extricate him - Weidner urging him on - the Indians overtook him and killed him. One continued to follow

Weidner. Henry stopped, took deliberate aim, and made him bite the dust. He killed him with that same old gun whose barrel was about six feet long and was brought from Pennsylvania when he first came to North Carolina.

He returned to South Carolina and remained there, in all, about two years, and they all returned to their homes, and were never afterwards molested on account of the Indians.

Mrs. Mull, nee Poff, the beautiful and charming widow, after a few years laid aside her weeds of mourning and married Major George Wilfung. They were blessed with two sons and four daughters. They all raised large and respectable families. When Henry Weidner and Mrs. Mull returned, this giant oak whose trunk measures twenty-two feet around, and whose branches extend far and wide, and afford shelter for this vast audience, was a small tree and was painted red as a warning that the war still continued.

After Henry Weidner led the way, he was followed by the Hokes, Conrads, Reinhardts, Anthonys, Frys, Forneys, Raachs, Ramsuers, Doyles, Bosts, Shufords, Summerows (Summerours) Dellingers, Sigmons and a number of other families, who, take them all in all, are a noble set of people. They built their homes over springs and in case of siege of the Indians, they could have water to drink with loopholes in the rock walls from which to shoot their assailants. There is an evidence of this fact in sight in the old dwelling house of the great pioneer, Henry Weidner. They carried their lives in their hands, not knowing at what time they would be shot down by an Indian in ambush or lurking behind some convert wall. We often think we live in evil times, but the blessings we enjoy can't be enumerated, compared to those of our fore fathers. On the 20th of March 1633, King Charles, the Second, granted to Edward, Earl of Clarendon, and others as true and absolute Lord Proprietors of all the country from the Atlantic to the Pacific ocean included between the 31st and 36 parallels, North latitude; and on the 3Oth of June, 1665, by a second charter, he enlarged the powers of the grantees, and extended their boundaries so as to include all the country between the parallels, 36 degrees and 30 minutes and 30 degrees, north latitude. On the 25th day of July 1729, seven of the eight proprietors of the Carolinas in consideration of 50 pounds of Sterling, conveyed all their rights, privileges, and franchises to George the II, King of the great Britain, and Ball Cararet, afterwards, Lord Granville, afterward, conveyed all his rights of jurisdiction over the said province or colony, reserving one-eighth part of the soil in North Carolina from the Virginia line south to 35 degrees, 35 minutes and from the Atlantic to the Pacific Ocean, a magnificent domain. This line was not defined west of the Catawba River until 1835, and consequently, a large number of grants were taken out in the name of the King north of that line during the period from 1720 to 1782.

Henry Weidner's Grant of 1750

Henry Weidner's grant to this splendid plantation was taken out in 1750 in the name of the King. The date of the Rock House place was taken out in 1750 in the same way. The other Plantations belonging to Henry Weidner along these two beautiful rivers were patented afterwards. He had three sons and five daughters. The names of the sons are Daniel, Henry and Abram. The latter was killed during the Revolutionary War. He had five daughters whose names were: Mary, who married Lightfoot Williams; Barbara, who married John Dellinger; Elizabeth, who married Henry Summerow (...Summerour...); Catherine, who married John Muell (commonly called M-U-L-L); Mollie, who married Jesse Robinson. He gave his son Henry the Rock House place, who hid it about twenty-five years and then he sold it to Jacob Summey and moved to the state of Missouri and there died. One of his sons told Dr. Fox who visited him in Missouri, that if he had the Rock House place back, he wouldn't give it for half the state of Missouri. To Daniel, he gave the Darius Sides' place near where the late George Weidner lived. He lived and died on this place and left a large number of respectable and well to do descendants and was buried in the old family graveyard on yonder hill near by. To his daughter Mary, he gave the place now owned by Major Mull, Esq., and was known as the Lightfoot Williams place. Elizabeth, he gave a part of the Mull land. To Catherine, he gave the lands occupied by the Mulls on Jacob's Fork.

He deeded his home place to Jesse Robinson, his son-in-law, instead of his daughter Mollie. The Dellinger place he devised in this last will and testament to his grandchildren, John Dillinger, Jr., Henry Dellinger, who was killed in the battle of Kings' Mountain, Joseph Dellinger, Catherine Dellinger, and Barbara Dellinger, the children of his son-in-law John Dellinger. He owned besides these splendid plantations, and with that he gave away by deed, about ten thousand acres. He was called the "King of the Forks". Time has attested his superior judgment in the choice of his lands. He was truly a Saxon. It is said they want all the lands that join them. Why it was that he gave this place to Jesse Robinson instead of his daughter Mollie, no one knows. It is supposed that he agreed to support his father and mother-in-law during their lives, he having married the youngest daughter. It has fallen into good and safe hands. It soon came into the possession of Henry Weidner Robinson, who was a relative of Henry Weidner's children. No better man could have owned it. He was a friend of the poor and needy. He distributed his bounty with a liberal hand. He was greatly beloved by all his neighbors. He lived to a good and ripe old age and died without an enemy. The crowning act of his life (by the pious example of his noble and Christian wife, when the sacrament of the Lord's supper was being administered to her for the last time in his presence by the Rev. John Fritchey, who saw that he wanted to unite with her in celebrating the dying love of his Savior, asked him if he, too, did not want to give himself to Jesus, and he said he did) was joining the church; then the Reverend minister administered the sacrament to both. A large portion of these magnificent domains are in the hands of the descendants of this great pioneer, who for honesty, integrity, and correct living, is not surpassed by any kindred of any people. The descendants of Henry Weidner should be proud of their record. They have showed themselves equal to every emergency; naturally modest and unobtrusive, but when occasion required, they were bold and daring.

Henry's son Daniel shoots Col. Ferguson at King's Mountain with Henry's Musket

Daniel Weidner, the eldest son of Henry Weidner, when the time came for him to defend his country and fight for liberty, shouldered his musket and volunteered under Colonel McDowell. He was one of the heroes of the Battle of King's Mountain. It was one of the most decisive battles and one of the grandest victories that was ever achieved by any people. It was the turning point in the great Revolution. A battle in which more that fifty of the enemy were slain and the rest captured. So there was not one left to tell Cornwallis of the disastrous defeat of Colonel Ferguson, that daring and blood thirsty leader.

It was Daniel Weidner's gun that gave Colonel Ferguson one of the mortal wounds with which he died on the spot. The late George Summey, Esq., a man of high character, known for integrity, told the Mon. S.T. Wilfong that as he (...Daniel...) took as deliberate aim at Ferguson as he ever did at a buck, and when his gun fired, Ferguson fell. [Editors Note: Many, many bullets went into Ferguson in very rapid sequence, and there was much dispute over who fired the fatal shot]

That same gun was brought by Henry Weidner from Pennsylvania; its barrel was half rifled, and about six feet long and carried an ounce ball, and by the patriotism of Peter Wilfong, was donated to the Guilford Battle Ground Company, and there placed among the Revolutionary relics in honor of the noble deed of Daniel Weidner. Not far from Daniel Weidner in this battle, his neighbor, friend and brother-in-law, young John Wilfong, received a severe wound in the right arm that same and glorious fight and carried that honorable scar to his grave. He afterwards became a great man in wealth, popularity, and good deeds. He never sought political office, not withstanding he was chosen elector on the Van Buren ticket and was made chairman of that college, where the great Nathaniel Macon was his colleague to cast the vote of that body. He is honored on the Gilford Battleground by that patriotic company. A beautiful lake on that sacred spot is named in his honor, Wilfong Lake" These two men fought under Major Joe McDowell in the Burke and Rutherford Regiments, together with John Dellinger and others in the King's Mountain battle. All the territory of Catawba County then belonged to Burke County as far south as Earl Gransville's line for that was the dividing line, at that time, between Burke and Ryan counties. The annea of these three brave patriots are not mentioned in Draper's History of King Mountain and Its Heroes

Young Wilfong, on his way home from the battle (he was discharged near Wilkesboro and crossed the Catawba River near the Island Ford) - - about 6 miles from the river, was weary and worn down making his way home, came to the house of Captain Paulzer Sigmon who lived at Lyle's Creek, on the old place owned by the late Logan Dellinger, Esq. He stopped to get a drink of water, for he was badly wounded. Captain Sigmon called his daughter Hannah, a stripling girl of sweet sixteen, to bring the young man some water from the spring. She almost flew as she went and came. She was as fair as a lily, her cheeks as a rose, her hair like shining gold. He stayed and rested all night. He left next morning. He loved Hannah at first sight. After the war was over, they became husband and wife. They raised a large and respectable family of children. They acquired a large amount of property. Our host here today, John W. Robinson, is one of the descendants of that union. No man can ever say that Henry Weidner ever did a dishonorable thing. He stood high among his fellow countrymen. He sold his friend, Conrad Yoder, a magnificent farm for small price, to have him as a neighbor. They continued fast friends as long as they lived, and his descendants and Conrad Yoder's are here today to rise up and praise him.

Henry Weidner's Will [2]

A short time before he died, Henry Weidner made his last will and testament in writing. It is always interesting to hear the last words of the deceased friend. He disposed of all his valuable land except the Dellinger place before he died. He was to a great degree his own executor. He did not (like too many) hold on to his property till he could hold it no longer, then give it away to his children. \

.~.

Henry Weidner was a bold, daring, brave man, who was not afraid of the Indians tomahawk

---

[2] This man was known as Wettiner, Weidner, Whitener, Whitner. Englishmen had trouble with his name, but he is well documented as the same an.

or scalping knife, but was willing to sacrifice his life for his posterity and generations unborn. The time was when we could not easily get marble to tell where our beloved ones lie. That time has passed. Marble is easily had, besides, these hills are full of gray granite that will last as long as the eternal hills, where we may hew out shafts to reach high up toward Heaven and mark the spot where the noble dead lie. Where rest the bones of Daniel Whitener, the hero of Kings Mountain? Yes, sons and daughters of royal blood, his descendants, tell me where? If he lies in the neglected grave, come to the rescue. Let generations unborn know that he was one of the heroes of King's Mountain; that he and his posterity are worth of the good and brave pioneer, the first discoverer of this goodly land.

If our meeting her today does nothing more than to pass a few compliments over the dead heroes, then we will not have met in vain. It should do more than this. We all ought to resolve that we will do our duty in trying to raise from oblivion our deserted friends, who now lie in the cold silent grave. A pencil mark is worth more than all the memories of the world. The mark of the chisel on graphite or marble is worth more than all the pencil marks on earth. It will last until the heavens shall roll together, till this solid globe shall melt with fervent heat, and until there shall be a new heaven and a new earth. Until then and only then shall there be need of monuments and histories to preserve the virtues of our honored dead.

We are all passing through nature to eternity. In a short time, the plowshare will be turned up with the plowshare and bleached with the clod of the valley? Shall no loving hands strew flowers on our graves and shed a tear of memory over the sod that covers them? Forbid it, Heaven! Forbid it, my countrymen, that our graves should be thus neglected. If we neglect others, we may share the same fate. This small tablet at the head of Henry Weidner's grave is all that is left of this great man and his beloved wife.

Catherine Weidner (...she was born Maria Katarina Muell and became Mary Catherine Mull in the colonies...) was born May 24th, 1733, and died August 20th, 1804, aged seventy-one years; two months, and twenty-six days.

Henry Weidner (...born Heinrich Wettin and became known variously as Henry Wetner/Weidner/Whitener in the colonies...) was born in the year 1717, Oct. 9th and died July 21st, 1792, aged seventy-four years, eight months. He lies buried in yonder cemetery with only this humble stone to mark his grave. He deserves a monument whose top should be first to catch a glimpse of the rays of the rising sun and say to the generations unborn: 'Here lies one of nature's noblemen, an honor to his race and a blessing to his country..'"

The Colonial American Indian Wars

The Colonial American Indian Wars caused great dissension. The descendants of my family's Weidner/ Summerour/ Wininger/ Moore lines have Native American - Cherokee / Choctaw - lines, added in America's history, on the Wininger line and the Hines lines which goes into Moore. Porter Kalvin Wininger was one fourth Cherokee and Susan Caroline Hines, whose grandmother was a Cherokee woman, whose Christian name was Mary Campbell was born and living on the Eastern Cherokee Reservation at the time of her marriage to Caleb Goodman, and 4th generation American who was ethnically full blood German. . Susan Caroline, who was one fourth Cherokee/Choctaw married Enoch Moore. And so Americans become one people, we shall hope! The speakers in this era seem to us biased toward their own Anglo-Saxon heritage and disparaging of the native cultures, a result without doubt of the strife mentioned later in the narrative where bloody clashes with marauding Cherokee Warriors left pioneer babies scalped and dying beside their dead father.

Even today, Cherokees still talk about the Trail of Tears leading from lands in Georgia given them by the Great White Father till the rivers run dry" to Oklahoma Territory reservations for the survivors of that terrible ordeal. Ironically, many Georgia Cherokees were Christianized farmers, and many were slave holders. Many Indians" had white blood and many "white colonials" had Indian blood, since intermarriage was common in Colonial times, particularly among the Cherokee. Cherokee land in Georgia was also the site of the nation's first gold strike, in Dahlonega, which means golden leaves (or money) in Cherokee; and some lashed back at pioneers invading their lands once again, after being moved from Virginia and the Carolinas, their original home.

Before we who descend from European Colonial ancestors become overwhelmed with guilt, let us reflect on the cruel territorial wars waged for centuries by Indian tribes before the arrival of the white man, and the territorial wars in Europe centuries before migration by Europeans to America, with much territory changing hands on both continents.

It was a cruel, hard era. Women were chattel, blacks (and the Irish vanquished in battle for that matter) were slaves and freedom for all men was meant to be for the white Anglo/Saxon land holding male, and in fact meant freedom from the rule of an absolute monarch. But freedom is contagious! All long for it, male and female of every race and creed, in every walk of life. In time it came to mean each and every one of us in the United States. To the degree that it is not yet perfect, we should strive toward perfection in generations to come.

Henry Weidner's Will:

This is his will:

In the name of God, Amen. The seventh day of December in the year of our Lord, 1790, I, Henry Weidner, Sr., of the County of Lincoln, in the state of North Carolina, planter, being sick and weak in body, but of perfect mind and memory, and calling to mind the mortality of my body, and knowing it is appointed for all men once to die, do make and ordain this my last will and testament in manner as follows. That is to say: In the first place, I give, devise and bequeath unto well-beloved wife, Catherine, a negro … named Phyllis; one hundred pounds in cash; her bed and furniture, while she remains single and no longer, a horse and saddle and spinning wheel, her privilege in the mansion house and all the household furniture. I give unto my son, Daniel, … I give unto my son Henry, …five negroes, viz.; Henry, Pete, Pleasant, David, and Nancy. I also will that my said two sons, Daniel and Henry have all my farm tools and utensils of husbandry, equally divided between them; Daniel to have the first choice and Henry the second and so to continue by choice until they have the whole. I give unto my daughter Mary, five cows, a negro … named Fanny, and her bed and furniture. I give unto my daughter Catherine, wife of John Mull, a negro named Nancy. I also give unto my daughter Barbara, wife of John Dellenger, a debt of seventy-five pounds. I also give unto daughter Elizabeth, wife of Henry Summeror / Summerour) debt of seventy-five pounds. likewise give unto my daughter, Mollie, a certain debt of sixty-six pounds, my two stills and all the still vessels, and a horse now in her possession. I also will that if any or part of my movable estate not particularly disposed of should remain in the hands of my executors, it all be equally divided among all my children, male and female.

also give, devise, and bequeath unto John Dellinger, Jr., and Barbara Dellinger, the children of my son-in-law and his wife, my daughter, Barbara, the certain tract of land whereon said John Dellinger now lives situated on Jacob's Fork, being a part of sundry surveys and containing by estimation 400 acres, be the same more or less. And lastly I make, nominate, constitute and appoint my loving and dutiful sons, Daniel and Henry Weidner, my whole and sole executors of this my last will and testament, ratifying and confirming this and no other to be my last will and testament. In testimony whereof I have hereunto interchangeably set my hand and affixed my seal, the year above written

Henry Weidner (Seal)

Signed and sealed by the testator, as and for his last will and testament, in the presence of us, who were present at the signing and sealing thereof.

Robert Blackburn

Michael Shell

John (X) Mull

Land is inherited

The land left by this Henry to his daughter, Elizabeth, before he made his will was given by her husband, Henry Summerour to his two sons, Henry and John Summerour. They sold it, and moved to Walton County, Georgia, (not far from Atlanta) where John's son, Berry Summerour and Berry's daughter, Susan were born. Berry Summerour served in the CSA in the Georgia forces. After the end of the Civil War, he left Georgia for the "West" sometime after 1873. The family was settled in Grayson, County Texas by 1880, where Berry J. Summerour, a farmer, is listed with his family in the census. In Texas, Susan, in 1885 at about 25, married Porter Kalvin Wininger, a widower with three children. Porter and Susan lived in Montague County Texas by 1900. Porter and Susan (Summerour) Wininger's first four children were daughters, three of whom married (3) brothers, members of the neighboring Moore family

Susan is this author's Great-Grandmother, whom my father wished me to be named after as well as his other grandmother, Susan Caroline Hines.
.

Georgia born Susan Mae Summerour became a Texan living in Grayson County by 1880 at the age of fourteen, living in a county not far from the Red River, the border of southern Oklahoma. .There, not many miles away in Wise County, Texas, her daughter Elizabeth Wininger married Enoch Moore, whose first child was my father, Harlen E. Moore. Just as Harlen reached manhood the Moore's followed the oil boom to Oklahoma, where Harlen met his wife, Della Lee Peck whose Great-Grandgrandfather Adam Peck II, or "Adam the Younger" had also been a goldminer in Dahlonega, Lumpkin County, Georgia. .

The Descendants of the German Pioneers to North Carolina

The following descendant reports were sent from many sources, and meant to be used as guidelines, since most cannot be verified by this author.

This Authors Proven Direct Line of Descent from Henry Whitner PS, NC and Henry Summerour, Militia, NC

I can verify my own direct line down Henry Whitner, Revolutionary Patriot of North Carolina and his son-in-law Henry Summerour II, whose Patriot service I was the first to prove conclusively to the satisfaction of the Daughters of the American Revolution. I hold a patriot bar among the seven on my DAR ribbon for these two patriots. This proof was possible because I discovered a land record given only to Revolutionary War veterans for payment for their service to aid in the founding of the United States of America.

Professor Deal, docent at Kings Mountain National Park

I also spoke with a Professor Deal at King Mountain National Park who served as docent in the summer and a college professor in the winter. He was a descendant of some of the Germans who joined the pioneers to North Carolina, the Diehl family. He told me *"every able bodied many in Lincoln County, North Carolina served as either a Revolutionary Patriot to found the United States or as a Tory to aid Ferguson and the English to keep America as a British Colony."* Professor Deal added *"the women went with their men to the Kings Mountain battle, to avoid attack and slaughter at home by the Indian allies of the British. They stood behind their men, loading the long rifles, with babies slung on their backs and toddlers clinging to their skirts. When their men fell, they picked up their husbands rifle and continued to fire."*

Two Reports of Some Descendants of the German Pioneers to North Carolina

See the following pages for
*a 4 Generation Descent for Henry Wettiner/Weidner/Whitener – who the NS DAR lists as Henry Whitner
*a 6 Generation Descent for Henry Summerour II, a "newly proven" Revolutionary Patriot on the line of Susan Moore Teller and some of her "cousins' contributed by various correspondents.

4 Generation Descendant Report for Henry The Saxon

1 Heinrich Wettin >Henry Whitener|Weidner RV WR (1717 - 1792) b: 09 Oct 1717 in Coberg, Saxony, Germany, d: 21 Sep 1792 in (what is now), Lincoln Co, NC
  + Maria Katharina Muehle (1733 - 1804) b: 24 May 1733 in Berks Co PA, m: 24 Oct 1751, d: 20 Aug 1804 in (now Lincoln Co), Catawba Co NC
  ...2 Daniel Weidner|Whitener (1751 - 1833) b: 14 Oct 1751 in Lincoln Co., NC, d: 08 Jan 1833
    + Mary Wilfong (about 1764 -) b: Abt. 1764 in NC, m: Aft. 1780 in Catawba Co., NC
    ......3 Daniel Weidner|Whitener
        + Polly Robinson b: Catawba Co NC
      ....4 Henry Weidner|Whitener
      ....4 Sally Weidner|Whitener
      ....4 Mary Weidner|Whitener
      ....4 Daniel Weidner|Whitener
      ....4 Jessee Weidner|Whitener
      ....4 Peter Weidner|Whitener
      ....4 Leah Weidner|Whitener
    ......3 Henry Weidner|Whitener
    ......3 John Weidner|Whitener
    ......3 George Weidner|Whitener
    ......3 David Weidner|Whitener
    ......3 Sally Weidner|Whitener
    ......3 Rachel Weidner|Whitener
    ......3 Mary Weidner|Whitener
    ......3 Betsy Weidner|Whitener
    ......3 Catherine Weidner|Whitener
  ...2 Henry Whitener, Jr. (1752 - 1811) b: 1752 in Lincolnton, Lincoln, NC, USA, d: 1811 in Marquand, Madison, MO, USA
    + Mary Catherine Schell (1770 - 1822) b: 29 Jun 1770 in Lancaster, Lancaster, Pennsylvania, USA, m: 1786 in Lincolnton, Lincoln, North Carolina, USA, d: 1822 in Marquand, Madison, Missouri, USA
    ......3 Catherine Whitener (1782 - 1844) b: 1782 in Lincolnton, Lincoln, North Carolina, United States, d: 01 Sep 1844 in Castor, Bollinger, Missouri, United States
    ......3 Barbara Whitener (1785 - 1864) b: 1785 in Lincolnton, Lincoln, North Carolina, United States, d: 1864 in Marble Hill, Bollinger, Missouri, United States
    ......3 Charity Whitener (1786 - 1840) b: 1786 in Lincoln, North Carolina, United States, d: 1840 in Bollinger, Missouri, United States
    ......3 Henry Whitener, III (1787 - 1864) b: 24 Apr 1787 in Lincolnton, Lincoln, North Carolina, USA, d: 17 Nov 1864 in Cape Girardeau, CO, MO
    ......3 Solomon Whitener (1794 - 1871) b: 05 Oct 1794 in North Carolina, United States, d: 08 Dec 1871 in Bollinger, Missouri, United States
    ......3 Benjamin Whitener (1803 - 1863) b: 09 Feb 1803 in Catawba, North Carolina, United States, d: Jan 1863 in Madison, Missouri, United States
    ......3 Mary Whitener
    ......3 John Whitener Whitener, Jr.
    ......3 Abraham Whitener
  ...2 Mollie (Mollianna) Weidner|Whitener (1752 - 1796) b: 08 Aug 1752 in Lincolnton, Lincoln, NC, USA, d: 1796 in Catawaba, NC, USA
  ...2 Abram Weidner|Whitener (1754 - 1780) b: 1754 in NC, d: 07 Oct 1780 in Kings Mountain, SC
  ...2 Barbara Weidner|Whitener (1756 - 1840) b: 1756 in NC, d: 08 Feb 1840 in Lincoln, NC, USA
  ...2 Elizabeth Whitener|Weidner (1764 - 1827) b: 01 Jan 1764 in Anson Co., NC, d: 21 Oct 1827 in Lincolnton, Lincoln Co, NC
    + Henry Summerour II (1759 - 1836) b: 1759 in Catawba Co., NC; USA: Rev War Land Grant for service Kings Mountain, m: 08 Oct 1784 in Lincoln, North Carolina, United States, d: 1836 in Lincolnton, Lincoln, North Carolina, United States; Old White Church (now Emmanuel Lutheran)
    ......3 Elizabeth Summerour (1785 -) b: 1785 in Lincoln Co., NC
    ......3 Barbara Summerour (1785 -) b: 1785 in Lincoln Co., NC

   +Leir Shrum (1820 -) b: 1820 in NC
   +Wiley Hallman (1785 -) b: 1785, m: Bef. 1823 in Lincoln Co NC
.........4Anna Hallman (1823 -) b: 1823 in NC
.........4Alfred Hallman (1828 -) b: 1828 in Lincoln Co., NC
   +Mary Killian (1827 -) b: 1827
.........4Mary Jane Hallman (1828 -) b: 1828 in NC
   +Robert Boslick
.........4Amy 'Mamie' Hallman (1831 -) b: 1831 in NC
   +Leir Tucker
.........4Elizabeth 'Betsy' Hallman (1834 -) b: 1834 in NC
.........4Margaret Hallman (1836 -) b: 1836 in NC
.........4Sallie Hallman (1840 -) b: 1840 in NC
   +Giles Beal
.........4Catherin Hallman (1841 -) b: 1841
.........4Benjamin Franklin Hallman (1844 -) b: 1844 in NC
   +Martha Sherrell
.........4Isabella Hallman (1845 -) b: 1845 in NC
   +Cephase Keener
   +Albert Kerksey
.........4W. Miles Hallman (1858 -) b: 1858 in NC
   +Belzora Dellinger
......3Daniel Summerour (1787 - 1855) b: 28 Dec 1787 in Burke Co., NC, d: 15 Mar 1855 in Lincoln Co. NC
   +Elizabeth Gilbert (1788 -) b: 1788, m: Bef. 1810 in NC
.........4Henry Summerour 1810 (1810 - 1840) b: 1810 in NC, d: 1840
.........4Margaret Summerour 1813 (1813 -) b: 1813 in NC
   +Noah Dellinger (1814 -) b: 1814
.........4Daniel Summerour 1815 (1815 -) b: 1815 in NC
.........4Sarah 'Sally' Summerour (1819 -) b: 1819 in NC
   +John Gilbert
.........4George Summerour 1824 (1824 -) b: 1824
.........4Solomon Summerour (1828 - 1891) b: 1828 in NC, d: 1891
   +Louise Rudisill (1837 -) b: 1837
.........4Mary Summerour 1830 (1830 -) b: 1830 in NC
   +Emanual Poovey (1819 -) b: 1819
.........4Salome Summerour
   +Norris Wingate
......3Henry Summerour III (1788 - 1848) b: 12 Sep 1788 in NC, d: 12 Feb 1848 in Aurora, GA
   +Sarah Salome Sietz (1790 - 1843) b: 20 Jul 1790 in NC, m: Bef. 1811, d: 1843 in GA
.........4Harrison Summerour (1814 - 1888) b: 1814 in Lincolnton, Lincoln Co, S.C., d: 1888 in Warsaw, Fulton Co., GA
   +Mary Ann Henderson (1827 - 1911) b: 1827, m: Bef. 1850 in GA, d: 1911
.........4Benjamin Franklin Summerour (1817 - 1874) b: 1817 in Lincolnton, Lincoln Co, S.C., d: 1874 in GA
   +Addaline Speller (1823 - 1865) b: 1823, m: Bef. 1842, d: 1865 in GA
   +Olilie Philippine Caroline Muller (1831 - 1877) b: 1831, m: Bef. 1868 in Terrell Co., GA, d: 1877
.........4Michael DeKalb Summerour (1819 - 1828) b: 1819, d: 1828
.........4Susannah Summerour (1823 -) b: 1823 in GA
.........4John Lafayette Summerour (1829 - 1887) b: 28 May 1829 in Walton, Georgia, United States, d: 26 Dec 1887 in Dawson, Georgia, United States
   +Amelda Spriggs (1832 - 1908) b: 1832, m: 07 Oct 1847 in Lumpkin Co., GA, d: 1908
   +Ameldia Spriggs (1832 - 1908) b: 05 Sep 1832 in Saluda Valley, Greenville, South Carolina, United States, m: 07 Oct 1847 in ,Lumpkin,Georgia,USA, d: 10 Oct 1908 in Dawson, Georgia, United States
.........4Anna Maria Summerour b: GA

............+Allen Mathews
......3Catherine Summerour (about 1790 -) b: Abt. 1790 in NC
.........+Tapster David Finger m: Bef. 1810 in Lincoln Co NC
.........4Susan Finger (1810 -) b: 1810 in Lincoln Co NC
............+George A. Ikard (1807 -) b: 1807
.........4Annie Finger (1812 -) b: 1812 in Lincoln Co., NC
............+Anthony Ikard (1815 -) b: 1815
.........4Frances Finger (1813 - 1886) b: 1813 in Lincoln Co NC, d: 1886
............+James Kistler
.........4Malinda Finger (1815 - 1846) b: 1815 in Lincoln Co NC, d: 1846
............+Henry Thornton
.........4Elizabeth Finger (1817 - 1843) b: 1817 in Lincoln Co NC, d: 1843
............+Elisha Ramsour
.........4Sallie Finger (1821 - 1854) b: 1821 in Lincoln Co NC, d: 1854
............+William Henson (1816 -) b: 1816
......3John Summerour (1792 - 1867) b: 1792 in Lincolnton, Lincoln Co, NC, d: 1867 in Between, Walton Co., GA
.........+Margaret "Peggy" Berry (1797 - 1875) b: 1797 in North Carolina, United States; 1880 US Census Walton Co GA - said born 1797, m: 22 Dec 1817 in Lincoln Co NC; marriage bond, d: 01 Jul 1875 in died bef 1876, Walton Co Georgia; bef 1876 Walton Co GA. per GA Tax Digest 1871-1876, son Berry administrator of her estate, i.e. she died before 1876. Her tombstone in Alcovy Cemetery says" Unkown Birth and Death Dates.
.........4Ezekial Summerour (1818 - 1894) b: 15 Nov 1818 in North Carolina, United States, d: 19 Jul 1894 in Henagar, DeKalb Co., Alabama, USA; Burial: Unity Baptist Missionary Cemetery, Henagar, DeKalb Co., Alabama, USA
............+Sarah Jane Sartor (1832 - 1919) b: 05 Aug 1832 in Hall Co., Georgia, USA, m: 22 Nov 1849 in Georgia, USA, d: 26 Mar 1919 in Henagar, DeKalb Co., Alabama, USA; Burial: Unity Baptist Missionary Cemetery, Henagar, DeKalb Co., Alabama, USA
.........4John Summerour Jr. 1823 (1823 - 1865) b: 03 May 1823 in NC, d: 1865 in Walton, Georgia, USA
............+Nancy Vineyard (1831 - 1857) b: 1831 in Georgia; 1850USCN-WaltonCoGA:ag 19, i.e. born circa 183, m: 19 Dec 1848 in Gwinnett, Georgia, USA, d: 1857 in Walton, Georgia, United States; died in childbirth: George Stephen Summerour.
............+Mary Carter (1833 -) b: May 1833 in Georgia, USA, m: 07 Dec 1858 in Oglethorpe, Georgia, USA
.........4Berry J Summerour (1829 - 1905) b: 10 Nov 1829 in Walton, Georgia, USA, d: 10 Feb 1905 in Selma, Montague, Texas, United States
............+Mary L. "Polly" Vineyard (1832 - 1922) b: 19 Aug 1832 in GA, per 1860 GA CN-+Death Certific-1922, m: 26 Nov 1850 in Gwinnett Co GA; by John W. Matthes: GA Marriage Records from Select Counties, 1828-1978, d: 29 Jul 1922 in Selma, Montague, Texas, United States
.........4Cynthia Summerour (1830 - 1890) b: 1830, d: 1890 in Milledgeville, Baldwin, Georgia, USA
............+Wiley Panel (1826 -) b: 1826, m: Georgia, USA; Y;Y;Y, d: Y
.........4Elizabeth Summerour (1832 - 1915) b: 1832 in Walton, Georgia, United States, d: 15 Feb 1915 in Newton, Georgia, United States; Buried in Macedonia Cemetery Oxford GA
............+Joe George
.........4William Summerour (1834 - after 1850) b: 1834 in GA, d: Aft. 1850 in Walton Co., GA census 1850
.........4Margaret Summerour (1836 - after 1850) b: 1836 in GA, d: Aft. 1850 in 1850 Walton, GA census.
............+Henry Briscoe
.........4Daniel Summerour c. 1827 b: Walton Co., GA
......3Mary Summerour (about 1794 -) b: Abt. 1794 in NC
.........+David Finger (1794 - 1871) b: 1794, m: Bef. 1820, d: 1871
.........4Levi Finger (1820 -) b: 1820
.........4Henry Finger (1822 -) b: 1822
.........4Solomon Finger (1827 -) b: 1827
.........4Sarah 'Sally' Finger (1828 -) b: 1828
.........4Susan Finger

.........4James Franklin Finger
......3Tapster Jacob Summerour (about 1801 -) b: Abt. 1801 in NC
    +Barbara Hallman (1801 -) b: 1801
.........4Elizabeth Summerour (1832 - 1915) b: 1832 in Walton, Georgia, United States, d: 15 Feb 1915 in Newton, Georgia, United States; Buried in Macedonia Cemetery Oxford GA
    +Joe George
.........4Margaret Summerour (1836 - after 1850) b: 1836 in GA, d: Aft. 1850 in 1850 Walton, GA census.
    +Henry Briscoe
.........4Adaline Summerour
.........4Susan Summerour
.........4Rochelle Summerour
.........4Rosanna Summerour
.........4Mary Summerour
......3Anna Summerour (1805 -) b: 1805 in NC
    +Lewis Keener (1805 - 1904) b: 1805, m: Bef. 1842, d: 1904
.........4Mary E. Keener
.........4Susan R. Keener
.........4William A. Keener
.........4Henry F. Keener
......3Susan Summerour (about 1806 - 1895) b: Abt. 1806 in NC, d: 1895
    +Jonas Finger m: Bef. 1823
.........4Salome Finger
......3Sally Summerour (- about 1896) b: NC, d: Abt. 1896 in NC
...2Mary Weidner|Whitener (1765 - 1796) b: 31 Mar 1765 in Anson, NC, USA, d: 1796 in NC
...2Catherine Weidner|Whitener b: NC

6 Generation Descendant Report for Heinrich Henry Summerour

1 Heinrich Henry Summerour (1717 - 1795) b: 09 Oct 1717 in Sommerau, Ansbach, Bayern, Germany, d: Oct 1795 ; Lincoln Co., NC (per MIMI, web page, ANC.com)http://awt.ancestry.com/cgi-bin, Burial: Emmanuel Church, Lincolnton, NC

  +Mary (1722 - 1794) b: 25 Oct 1722, m: Dec 1749 in Philadelphia, PN, d: 1794 in Lincoln, North Carolina, United States; Age at Death: 72, Burial: Lincolnton, Lincoln County, North Carolina, USA, Occupation: w>H.SummerourSr.

...2 Elizabeth Summerour (1754 -) b: 1754

...2 Michael Summerour (1760 - 1848) b: 1760 in Lincoln Co. NC, d: 1848 in Lincoln Co NC, Burial: 1835 in Luthuren Ch. Cem., Lincolnton, NC

  +Katherine Klein (1769 - before 1820) b: 1769 in Catawba Co NC, m: 1788 in Lincoln, North Carolina, USA, d: Bef. 1820 in Catawba Co NC, Burial: Old Luthern Cem., Lincolnton, NC, Occupation: w>MSummerour1760

......3 Henry Summerour (1786 - 1849) b: 12 Sep 1786 in Lincoln,,North Carolina,USA, d: 03 Feb 1849 in Auraria,Lumpkin,Georgia,USA

  +Barbara Henry Occupation: MS; w>H.Summerour

  +Sarah Salome Seitz (1790 - 1843) b: 19 Jul 1790 in Lincoln City,Lincoln,North Carolina,USA, d: 11 Apr 1843 in Lincoln City,Lincoln,North Carolina,USA

.........4 John Lafayette Summerour (1829 - 1887) b: 28 May 1829 in Walton, Georgia, United States, d: 26 Dec 1887 in Dawson, Georgia, United States, Burial: 1887 in Dawson Co., GA, Occupation: m.Amelda Spriggs

  +Amelda Spriggs (1832 - 1908) b: 1832, m: 07 Oct 1847 in Lumpkin Co., GA, d: 1908, Occupation: m.JLSummerour

............5 William Franklin Summerour (1848 - 1920) b: 1848, d: 1920

  +Minerva Burt (1853 - 1877) b: 1853, m: Bef. 1869, d: 1877, Occupation: m.Wm.F.Summerour

...............6 Curtis James Summerour (1869 - 1920) b: 1869, d: 1920, Occupation: m.Exer Mincey

  +Exer Mincey (1872 - 1895) b: 1872, m: Bef. 1894, d: 1895, Occupation: m.C.J.Summerour

...............6 John Mark Summerour (1871 - 1939) b: 1871, d: 1939, Occupation: m.Lona Goss

  +Lona Goss (1874 - 1939) b: 1874, d: 1939, Occupation: m.J.M.Summerour

  +Louisa Roberts (1849 - 1898) b: 1849, m: Bef. 1879, d: 1898, Occupation: 2wWm.F.Summerour

...............6 Robert Summerour (1879 - 1959) b: 1879, d: 1959, Occupation: never married

  +Florence N. Whitamore (1874 - 1963) b: 1874, m: Bef. 1902, d: 1963, Occupation: 3wWm.F.Summerour

...............6 Richard Homer Summerour (1902 - 1959) b: 1902, d: 1959, Occupation: m.Gertie Ingram

  +Gertie Ingram (1920 - 1974) b: 1920, m: Bef. 1935, d: 1974, Occupation: m.R.H.Summerour

...............6 Susan Summerour (1903 - 1910) b: 1903, d: 1910, Occupation: died young

...............6 Annie Lou Summerour (1904 - 1942) b: 1904, d: 1942, Occupation: m.Grady Stone

...............6 Henry Clay Summerour (1906 - 1978) b: 1906, d: 1978, Occupation: m.Irma Seay

6 Generation Descendant Report for Heinrich Henry Summerour

+Emily Irene Seay (1914 -) b: 1914, m: Bef. 1931, Occupation: m.Noel Summerour

....5John Henry Summerour (1854 - 1920) b: 1854 in GA, d: 1920, Occupation: m.Marg.Mathews
   +Margaret Matthews (1851 - 1914) b: 1851, m: Bef. 1874, d: 1914, Occupation: m.J.H.Summerour
......6Julia Elaine Summerour (1874 - 1965) b: 1874, d: 1965, Occupation: m.Gold Dale
   +Gold Dale (1871 - 1932) b: 1871, m: Bef. 1896, d: 1932, Occupation: m.J.E.Summerour
......6William Franklin Summerour (1876 - 1940) b: 1876, d: 1940, Occupation: m.Flor.Gillespie
   +Florence E. Gillespie (1891 -) b: 1891, m: Bef. 1914, Occupation: m.Wm.F.Summerour
......6John Lafayette Summerour (1879 - 1925) b: 1879, d: 1925, Occupation: m1.Davis2.Reed
   +Emma Davis (1875 - 1925) b: 1875, m: Bef. 1904, d: 1925, Occupation: m.J.L.Summerour
......6Zed Williford Summerour (1881 - 1924) b: 1881, d: 1924, Occupation: m.Verdie Pinson
......6Charles Henry Summerour (1883 - 1965) b: 1883, d: 1965, Occupation: m.Azzie Norrell
   +Azzie Lee Norrell (1890 - 1971) b: 1890, m: Bef. 1909, d: 1971, Occupation: m.C.H.Summerour
......6Pulaski Summerour (1883 - 1889) b: 1883, d: 1889, Occupation: died young
......6Susan Summerour (1885 - 1885) b: 1885, d: 1885, Occupation: infant death
......6Annie Louise Summerour (1889 - 1968) b: 1889, d: 1968, Occupation: m.John Dale
   +John N. Dale m: Bef. 1909, Occupation: m.AnnieSummerour
......6David Allen Summerour (1889 - 1968) b: 1889, d: 02 Jan 1968 in Aurora, Lumpkin Co., GA, Burial: Jan 1968 in Lumpkin Co., GA, Occupation: m.Eliz.Dale
   +Elizabeth Dale (1890 - after 1968) b: 1890, m: Bef. 1907, d: Aft. 1968, Occupation: m.Dave Summerour
......6Ameldia Viola Summerour (1891 -) b: 1891, Occupation: m.T.W.Rogers
......6Kate Salome Summerour (1893 - 1979) b: 1893, d: 1979, Occupation: m.Van Woody
....5Charles Lafayette Summerour (1856 - 1919) b: 1856 in GA, d: 1919, Occupation: m.MattieBearden
....5Thomas Iverson Summerour (1859 - 1941) b: 15 Dec 1859 in Dawson, Georgia, USA, d: 15 Jun 1941
   +Sara L Thompson (- 1900) b: GA, m: Bef. 1890 in GA, d: 1900, Occupation: 1w.TI Summerour
......6Mary Elizabeth Summerour (1891 -) b: 1891 in GA
......6Ruth Summerour (1893 -) b: 1893 in GA, Occupation: m.Jasper Cagle
......6Franklin Summerour (- 1915) b: GA, d: 1915, Occupation: m.Miss Conner
   +Mary Emmaline Dodd (1870 - 1964) b: 04 Sep 1870 in Lumpkin, Georgia, USA, m: Aft. 1900 in GA, d: 24 Apr 1964 in Dawson, Georgia, USA

6 Generation   Descendant Report for Heinrich Henry Summerour

..............6Katie Lee Louella Summerour (1903 - 1982) b: 17 Jan 1903, d: 01 Mar 1982, Occupation: w.J.E.Clayton

    +Joseph Enoch Clayton Slayton (1894 - 1970) b: 1894 in GA, m: Bef. 1923 in GA, d: 1970 in GA, Occupation: M.KLL.Summerour

............5Susan Theodocia Summerour (1861 - 1931) b: 1861 in GA, d: 1931, Occupation: no children

............5Zion Ezekiel Summerour (1865 - 1938) b: 1865 in GA, d: 1938

    +Loucindy Southern (1874 - 1950) b: 1874, m: Bef. 1895 in GA, d: 1950, Occupation: w.Zion Summerour

..............6Martha Loucindy Summerour (1895 - 1978) b: 1895 in GA, d: 1978, Occupation: m.E.ZekeWaters

..............6Daniel Joseph Summerour (1897 - 1955) b: 1897 in GA, d: 1955

..............6Mildred Marshall Summerour (1899 - 1978) b: 1899, d: 1978, Occupation: m.JamesRhindress

..............6Charles Henry Summerour (1903 -) b: 1903 in GA, Occupation: m.LillieAdamson

..............6Nurnil Grace Summerour (1905 -) b: 1905 in GA, Occupation: m.FrnklnSanders

..............6Kittie Sue Summerour (1909 -) b: 1909 in GA, Occupation: m.CarlosPierce

............5Jamus Robert Lee Summerour (1867 - 1936) b: 1867 in GA, d: 1936, Occupation: m.Sarah O.Rogers

............5Daniel Alexander Summerour (1869 - 1936) b: 1869 in GA, d: 1936, Occupation: m.Dora Brown

............5Beverly Nathaniel Summerour (1874 - 1949) b: 1874 in GA, d: 1949, Occupation: m.Amanda Mathews

    +Ameldia Spriggs (1832 - 1908) b: 05 Sep 1832 in Saluda Valley, Greenville, South Carolina, United States, m: 07 Oct 1847 in ,Lumpkin,Georgia,USA, d: 10 Oct 1908 in Dawson, Georgia, United States

............5Thomas Iverson Summerour (1859 - 1941) b: 15 Dec 1859 in Dawson County, Ga, d: 15 Jun 1941 in Dawson County, Ga

    +Mary Emmaline Dodd (1870 - 1964) b: 04 Sep 1870 in Lumpkin, Georgia, USA, d: 24 Apr 1964 in Dawson, Georgia, USA

..............6Katie Lee Louella Summerour (1903 - 1982) b: 17 Jan 1903 in Forsyth County, Georgia, d: 01 Mar 1982 in Dawsonville, Dawson, Georgia, United States

........3Jacob Summerow (1797 - 1889) b: 15 Jul 1797 in Lincoln, North Carolina, d: 02 Nov 1889 in Mitchell, North Carolina

........3David Summerour (about 1798 - 1879) b: Abt. 1798 in Lincoln Co., NC, d: 23 Jun 1879 in Lincoln, North Carolina, USA, Occupation: sonMichaelSumm.

    +Susannah Rudisill Occupation: w>David, Mich.son

..........4Henry Michael Summerour (1830 - 1926) b: 28 Feb 1830 in NC, d: 28 Sep 1926

    +Sarah Richards (1852 - 1924) b: 13 Apr 1852, m: 14 Dec 1871, d: 15 Apr 1924

............5Juanita Summerour (1873 -) b: 04 Mar 1873 in N C

............5Franklin Edward Summerour (1875 -) b: 19 Sep 1875 in NC

............5Thomas Summerour (1878 -) b: 17 May 1878 in NC

............5Willie Summerour (1888 -) b: 20 Aug 1888 in NC

6 Generation Descendant Report for Heinrich Henry Summerour

......3Elizabeth Summerour (1801 - 1861) b: 03 Aug 1801 in Lincoln Co., NC, d: 13 Jul 1861 in Lincoln, North Carolina, USA

......3Andrew Summerour (about 1803 - 1831) b: Abt. 1803 in Lincoln Co., NC, d: 1831 in Iredell, North Carolina, USA, Occupation: Michael's son

......3Michael P. Summerow (1805 - 1870) b: 1805 in Missouri, d: 05 May 1870 in Travis County, Onion Creek area, Texas

   +Electra (1807 - 1898) b: 1807 in MO, d: 16 Nov 1898 in Travis Co, TX

.........4Milton Summerour (about 1829 -) b: Abt. 1829 in AR

.........4Joel F. Summerour (about 1832 -) b: Abt. 1832 in AR

.........4Velena Summerour (about 1833 -) b: Abt. 1833 in AR

.........4Josephine M Summerour (about 1839 -) b: Abt. 1839 in AR

.........4Montarow Edward Summerour (1843 - after 1880) b: 1843 in AR, d: Aft. 1880 in TX

   +Sue Ann Black (1848 - 1877) b: 21 Feb 1848 in Arkansas, d: 05 Jun 1877 in Manchaca, Travis Co TX, Burial: 1877 in Live Oak Cemetery

............5Wm J Summerrow (1867 -) b: 1867

............5Robert E Summerrow (1868 - 1918) b: 23 Nov 1868 in TX, d: 22 Apr 1918

............5Sidney Summerrow (1869 - 1928) b: 1869 in TX, d: 19 Jun 1928 in Hays, TX

............5Edward Dallas Summerrow (1874 - 1937) b: 03 Aug 1874 in Austin, TX, d: 14 Feb 1937

   +Myrtle May Langley (1890 - 1979) b: 05 Feb 1890 in Temple, Bell, Texas, USA, d: 02 Feb 1979 in Austin, Travis, Texas, USA

...............6Earl J Summerrow (1918 - 1944) b: 03 Aug 1918 in Goose Creek, Harris, TX, d: 10 Nov 1944

   +Erma Grace Cude (1919 -) b: 02 Jun 1919 in Taylorsville, Caldwell, Texas, USA, m: 12 Oct 1938

   +Emma Baldwin (- 1914) d: 04 Dec 1914

...............6Eugene Bauldin Summerrow (1906 - 1971) b: 16 Mar 1906 in Hardin, TX, d: Jun 1971 in Houston, Harris, TX

......3Michael's son Jacob Summerour (about 1805 - 1889) b: Abt. 1805 in Lincoln Co., NC, d: 02 Nov 1889 in Mitchell, NC, Occupation: sonMichaelSum.

   +Rachel Zelpha Turner (1809 - 1888) b: 09 Aug 1809 in Lincoln, NC, USA, d: 30 Apr 1888 in Mitchell, NC

.........4Catherine Eliza Summerow (1833 -) b: 08 Dec 1833 in NC

.........4Sarah J Summerow (1835 -) b: 1835 in NC

.........4Elvira Elizabeth Summerow (1837 - 1905) b: 13 Feb 1837 in NC, d: 27 May 1905 in Mitchell, NC

.........4Jane Maria Summerow (1838 - 1915) b: 09 Nov 1838 in NC, d: 07 Jun 1915 in Avery, NC

.........4George Summerow (1840 -) b: 1840 in NC

.........4Peter Summerow (1842 -) b: 1842 in NC

.........4John Summerow (1844 -) b: 1844 in NC

.........4Jacob Wesley Summerrow (1846 - 1919) b: Sep 1846 in NC, d: 14 Mar 1919 in Avery, NC

.........4Amanda Summerow (1850 - 1926) b: 1850 in NC, d: 19 Feb 1926 in Banner Elk, Avery

6 Generation   Descendant Report for Heinrich Henry Summerour

.........4David Calvin Summerow (1852 -) b: 1852 in NC
......3Peter Summerour (1808 - 1841) b: 11 Dec 1808 in Lincoln Co., NC, d: 02 Nov 1841 in Lincoln, North Carolina, USA
   +Elvira Ramsrour b: NC, Occupation: w>Henry, Mich.son
......3Sarah "Sally" Summerour (1814 - 1841) b: Jan 1814 in Lincoln Co., NC, d: 22 Oct 1841 in Lincoln, North Carolina, USA
......3John Summerour Michael's son (- 1881) b: Lincoln Co., NC, d: 1881 in Iredell, North Carolina, USA, Occupation: Michael's son
...2Catherine Summerour (1757 -) b: 1757
...2Andrew Summerour (1758 -) b: 1758
...2Henry Summerour II (1759 - 1836) b: 1759 in Catawba Co., NC; USA: Rev War Land Grant for service Kings Mountain, Military Exper.: 07 Oct 1780 in Kings Mountain, Cleveland, North Carolina, USA; USA: Rev War Land Grant for service Kings Mountain - Accepted by DAR, d: 1836 in Lincolnton, Lincoln, North Carolina, United States; Old White Church (now Emmanuel Lutheran), Burial: Lincolnton, Lincoln County, North Carolina, USA

   +Elizabeth Whitener|Weidner (1764 - 1827) b: 01 Jan 1764 in Anson Co., NC, m: 08 Oct 1784 in Lincoln, North Carolina, United States, d: 21 Oct 1827 in Lincolnton, Lincoln Co, NC, Burial: Lincolnton, Lincoln Co, NC, Occupation: w>Hn.Summerour Jr
......3Elizabeth Summerour (1785 -) b: 1785 in Lincoln Co., NC, Occupation: spinster
......3Barbara Summerour (1785 -) b: 1785 in Lincoln Co., NC, Occupation: m.Ronald Ray
   +Leir Shrum (1820 -) b: 1820 in NC
   +Wiley Hallman (1785 -) b: 1785, m: Bef. 1823 in Lincoln Co NC
.........4Anna Hallman (1823 -) b: 1823 in NC, Occupation: w>LeirShrum
.........4Alfred Hallman (1828 -) b: 1828 in Lincoln Co., NC
   +Mary Killian (1827 -) b: 1827
.........4Mary Jane Hallman (1828 -) b: 1828 in NC
   +Robert Boslick
.........4Amy 'Mamie' Hallman (1831 -) b: 1831 in NC
   +Leir Tucker
.........4Elizabeth 'Betsy' Hallman (1834 -) b: 1834 in NC
.........4Margaret Hallman (1836 -) b: 1836 in NC
.........4Sallie Hallman (1840 -) b: 1840 in NC
   +Giles Beal
.........4Catherin Hallman (1841 -) b: 1841
.........4Benjamin Franklin Hallman (1844 -) b: 1844 in NC
   +Martha Sherrell
.........4Isabella Hallman (1845 -) b: 1845 in NC, Occupation: Kerksey; w>Keener
   +Cephase Keener
   +Albert Kerksey
.........4W. Miles Hallman (1858 -) b: 1858 in NC
   +Belzora Dellinger
......3Daniel Summerour (1787 - 1855) b: 28 Dec 1787 in Burke Co., NC, d: 15 Mar 1855 in Lincoln Co. NC

6 Generation Descendant Report for Heinrich Henry Summerour

+Elizabeth Gilbert (1788 -) b: 1788, m: Bef. 1810 in NC, Occupation: w>Dan.Summerour

.........4Henry Summerour 1810 (1810 - 1840) b: 1810 in NC, d: 1840, Occupation: m.Barbara:?:

.........4Margaret Summerour 1813 (1813 -) b: 1813 in NC, Occupation: w>Noah Dellinger
    +Noah Dellinger (1814 -) b: 1814

.........4Daniel Summerour 1815 (1815 -) b: 1815 in NC, Occupation: never married

.........4Sarah 'Sally' Summerour (1819 -) b: 1819 in NC, Occupation: w>John Gilbert
    +John Gilbert

.........4George Summerour 1824 (1824 -) b: 1824, Occupation: m.Emeline:?:

.........4Solomon Summerour (1828 - 1891) b: 1828 in NC, d: 1891, Occupation: m.LouiseRudisill
    +Louise Rudisill (1837 -) b: 1837

.........4Mary Summerour 1830 (1830 -) b: 1830 in NC, Occupation: w>Emanuel Poovey
    +Emanual Poovey (1819 -) b: 1819

.........4Salome Summerour Occupation: w>Norris Wingate
    +Norris Wingate

......3Henry Summerour III (1788 - 1848) b: 12 Sep 1788 in NC, d: 12 Feb 1848 in Aurora, GA, Burial: Auraria, Lumpkin County, Georgia, USA
   +Sarah Salome Sietz (1790 - 1843) b: 20 Jul 1790 in NC, m: Bef. 1811, d: 1843 in GA, Occupation: w>Hn.SumrIII

.........4Harrison Summerour (1814 - 1888) b: 1814 in Lincolnton, Lincoln Co, S.C., d: 1888 in Warsaw, Fulton Co., GA, Occupation: Grocer
   +Mary Ann Henderson (1827 - 1911) b: 1827, m: Bef. 1850 in GA, d: 1911

.............5John Henry Summerour (1850 - 1903) b: 1850 in Forsyth Co., Ga, d: 1903, Occupation: Merchant
    +Catherine Hope (1851 - 1905) b: 1851, m: Bef. 1871 in GA, d: 1905, Occupation: m.J.H.Summerour

................6Henry Harrison Summerour (1871 - 1954) b: 1871 in GA, d: 1954
    +Junia Rogers (1876 - 1970) b: 1876, m: Bef. 1894 in GA, d: 1970, Occupation: w>H.H.Summerour

................6Charles Anderson Summerour (1875 - 1953) b: 1875 in GA, d: 1953, Occupation: m.Anne Lewis
    +Annie E. Lewis (1887 - 1961) b: 1887, m: Bef. 1903, d: 1961, Occupation: m.C.A.Summerour

................6John Henderson Summerour (1877 - 1950) b: 1877 in GA, d: 1950, Occupation: m.Alma Mewborn
    +Alma E. Newborn (1882 - 1926) b: 1882, m: Bef. 1909, d: 1926

................6Frank Summerour (1884 - 1965) b: 1884, d: 1965, Occupation: m.Willa Little
    +Willa Mary Little (1890 - 1965) b: 1890, m: Bef. 1908, d: 1965, Occupation: m.FrankSummerour

................6Patrick W. Summerour (1890 - 1968) b: 1890 in GA, d: 1968, Occupation: m.Winni Little
    +Winnie N. Little (1892 - 1959) b: 1892, m: Bef. 1925, d: 1959

6 Generation   Descendant Report for Heinrich Henry Summerour

............6Guy Summerour (1893 - 1971) b: 1893 in GA, d: 1971, Occupation: never married
..........5Charles William Summerour (1857 - 1930) b: 1857 in Forsyth Co., Ga, d: 1930
   +Emma Heard (1865 - 1953) b: 1865, m: 24 Dec 1882, d: 1953, Occupation: m.C.W.Summerour
............6Susie Parilee Summerour (1885 -) b: 1885, Occupation: m.J.H.McGee
............6James Heard Summerour (1888 - 1958) b: 1888, d: 1958, Occupation: m.Lillie Lovett
............6Steven Harrison Summerour (1890 -) b: 1890, Occupation: m.Willie M.Knox
   +Willie Mae Knox (1890 -) b: 1890, Occupation: m.S.H.Summerour
............6Mary Ruth Summerour (1893 -) b: 1893, Occupation: m.Teasley Upshaw
............6Nellie Emma Summerour (1896 -) b: 1896, Occupation: never married
............6Charles William Summerour Jr. (1899 -) b: 1899, Occupation: Blanch Brinsfied
   +Emma Blanch Brinsfield (1901 -) b: 1901, m: 23 Nov 1927
............6Annie Kate Summerour (1901 - 1972) b: 1901, d: 1972, Occupation: m.Thurston Reese
............6Charlotte Summerour (1904 - 1968) b: 1904, d: 1968, Occupation: mJamesL.Crossley
..........5Thomas Ed Summerour (1859 - 1925) b: 1859 in Forsyth Co., Ga, d: 1925, Occupation: m.Annie Clark
..........5Jefferson Davis Summerour (1861 - 1932) b: 1861 in Forsyth Co., Ga, d: 1932, Occupation: m.Nannie Kelley
   +Nancy Kelley (1870 - 1939) b: 1870, m: Bef. 1893, d: 1939 in Vernon, Wilbarger Co., TX, Burial: Eastview, Memorial Park, Vernon TX, Occupation: m.J.D.Summerour
............6Thomas Jefferson Summerour (1893 - 1969) b: 1893, d: 1969 in Vernon, Wilbarger Co TX, Burial: Eastview, Memorial Park, Vernon TX
   +Sally Ish (1893 - 1927) b: 1893, m: Bef. 1918, d: 1927 in Bridgeport, Wise Co., TX, Occupation: 1w.TJSummerour
   +Ida Brown (1902 - 1957) b: 1902, m: Bef. 1929 in TX, d: 1957 in Bridgeport, Wise Co., TX, Burial: Bridgeport, Wise Co., TX, Occupation: 2w.TJSummerour
   +Delia Handley (- 1972) m: Aft. 1957, d: 1972 in Denver, Denver Co., CO, Occupation: 3wTJSummerour
..........5Mary A. Summerour (1863 - 1887) b: 1863 in Forsyth Co., Ga, d: 1887, Occupation: never married
..........5Homer Hightower Summerour (1866 - 1915) b: 1866 in Forsyth Co., Ga, d: 1915, Occupation: m.Susie Mitchum
   +Susie Mitchum (1869 - 1920) b: 1869, m: Bef. 1886, d: 1920, Occupation: m.HomerSummerour
............6Mary K. Summerour (1891 - 1916) b: 1891, d: 1916, Occupation: m.MarcusMashburn
............6Joseph Edwin Summerour (1905 -) b: 1905, Occupation: mEula Lee Fisher
   +Eula Lee Fisher (1905 -) b: 1905, m: Bef. 1930, Occupation: m.J.E.Summerour
............6Jeff H. Summerour Occupation: mAnnie Humphries
............6UNNAMED

> +Gradye Brooke (1889 - 1972) b: 1889, d: 1972, Occupation: m.B.F.Summerour
> +John Walker Wallace (about 1788 - 1846) b: Abt. 1788 in Virginia; `, d: 10 Nov 1846 in Lexington, Lafayette Co., MO, Burial: 10 Nov 1846 in Lexington, Lafayette Co, MO; Lexington Memory Gardens

........5 Susie E. Summerour (1869 - 1954) b: 1869 in Forsyth Co., Ga, d: 1954, Occupation: m.J.N.McClure

> +John N. McClure (1862 - 1927) b: 1862, m: Bef. 1888, d: 1927

............6 Robert Ed. McClure (1888 - 1977) b: 1888, d: 1977, Occupation: Medical Doctor
............6 Emma McClure (1890 - 1894) b: 1890, d: 1894
............6 Hallie McClure (1892 - 1960) b: 1892, d: 1960, Occupation: m.Guy Jones
............6 Annie McClure (1896 - 1950) b: 1896, d: 1950, Occupation: m.Ollie Simpson
............6 John Newton McClure (1899 -) b: 1899, Occupation: m.Mae Martz
............6 Mary McClure (1901 - 1974) b: 1901, d: 1974, Occupation: mWallaceStephens
............6 Katherine McClure (1905 - 1918) b: 1905, d: 1918
............6 Lois McClure (1908 -) b: 1908, Occupation: m.Harry Kinnett

......4 Benjamin Franklin Summerour (1817 - 1874) b: 1817 in Lincolnton, Lincoln Co, S.C., d: 1874 in GA, Occupation: bsman; goldminer

> +Addaline Speller (1823 - 1865) b: 1823, m: Bef. 1842, d: 1865 in GA, Occupation: m.B.F.Summerour

........5 Pulaski Lafayette Summerour (1842 - 1870) b: 1842 in Aurora, Lumpkin Co., GA, d: 1870

> +Mary E. Adair Occupation: m.P.L.Summerour

............6 Sarah Adaline Summerour Occupation: unknown husband
............6 Charles Franklin Summerour Occupation: no descendants

........5 Henry Harrison Summerour (1844 - 1846) b: 1844 in Aurora, Lumpkin Co., GA, d: 1846 in Aurora, Lumpkin Co., GA
........5 Jonathan Dekalb Summerour (1849 - 1849) b: 1849 in Aurora, Lumpkin Co., GA, d: 1849 in Aurora, Lumpkin Co., GA
........5 Sanford Guy Summerour (1852 - 1853) b: 1852 in Crandall, Murray Co., GA, d: 1853 in Crandall, Murray Co., GA
........5 Susan Ann Carolina Summerour (1853 - 1854) b: 1853 in Crandall, Murray Co., GA, d: 1854 in Crandall, Murray Co., GA
........5 Sarah Adaline Summerour (1856 - 1864) b: 1856 in Crandall, Murray Co., GA, d: 1864 in Dawson, Terrell Co., FL
........5 William Franklin Summerour (1858 - 1921) b: 1858 in Crandall, Murray Co., GA, d: 1921, Occupation: m.Maggie McCamy

> +Maggie McCamy (1860 - 1920) b: 1860, m: Bef. 1890, d: 1920, Occupation: m.Wm.F.Summerour

............6 Robert Pulaski Summerour (1882 - 1883) b: 1882, d: 1883, Occupation: infant death
............6 Maude Olilie Summerour (1884 - 1974) b: 1884, d: 1974, Occupation: m.Th.R.Jones

> +Thomas Richard Jones Jr. m: Bef. 1913, Occupation: mMaude Summerour

............6 William Frankin Summerour Jr. (1890 - 1948) b: 1890, d: 1948, Occupation: m.Lena Showalter

> +Lena Showalter m: Bef. 1910, Occupation: mW.F.SummerourJr

6 Generation Descendant Report for Heinrich Henry Summerour

............6Mildred Louise Summerour Occupation: m.Jimmy Walker

.........5Martha Salome Summerour (1860 - 1937) b: 1860 in Crandall, Murray Co., GA, d: 1937, Occupation: m.Wm. Gregory

+William Daily Gregory (1850 - 1920) b: 1850, m: Bef. 1878, d: 1920

............6Myra Adaline Gregory (1878 - 1974) b: 1878, d: 1974, Occupation: m.John W. Harris

+John W. Harris (1877 - 1934) b: 1877, m: Bef. 1899, d: 1934

............6Ora Claude Gregory (1882 - 1955) b: 1882, d: 1955, Occupation: m.Arthur Mullins

+Arthur Lee Mullins (1883 - 1971) b: 1883, m: Bef. 1905, d: 1971, Occupation: m.Ora Gregory

............6Nannie Sue Gregory (- 1912) d: 1912, Occupation: m.Emmet Stanley

............6Eugenia Evelyn Gregory (- 1975) d: 1975, Occupation: m.Dr.F.C.Bentley

+F. C. Bentley m: Bef. 1918, Occupation: Physician

............6Benjamin Franklin Gregory (- 1910) d: 1910

.........5Fannie Olilie Summerour (1863 - 1863) b: 1863 in Crandall, Murray Co., GA, d: 1863 in Crandall, Murray Co., GA

+Olilie Philippine Caroline Muller (1831 - 1877) b: 1831, m: Bef. 1868 in Terrell Co., GA, d: 1877, Occupation: 2w.BFSummerour

.........5Arabella Concordia Summerour (1868 - 1890) b: 1868 in Crandall, Murray Co., GA, d: 1890 in Crandall, Murray Co., GA

.........5Cohuttah Leona Summerour (1870 - 1896) b: 1870 in Crandall, Murray Co., GA, d: 1896, Occupation: m.CharlesT.Owens

+Charles T. 'Chip' Owens m: Bef. 1895, Occupation: m.C.L.Summerour

............6Felix Church Owens (1895 -) b: 1895

......4Michael DeKalb Summerour (1819 - 1828) b: 1819, d: 1828, Occupation: never married

......4Susannah Summerour (1823 -) b: 1823 in GA, Occupation: m.Wm.Hendrix

......4John Lafayette Summerour (1829 - 1887) b: 28 May 1829 in Walton, Georgia, United States, d: 26 Dec 1887 in Dawson, Georgia, United States, Burial: 1887 in Dawson Co., GA, Occupation: m.Amelda Spriggs

+Amelda Spriggs (1832 - 1908) b: 1832, m: 07 Oct 1847 in Lumpkin Co., GA, d: 1908, Occupation: m.JLSummerour

.........5William Franklin Summerour (1848 - 1920) b: 1848, d: 1920

+Minerva Burt (1853 - 1877) b: 1853, m: Bef. 1869, d: 1877, Occupation: m.Wm.F.Summerour

............6Curtis James Summerour (1869 - 1920) b: 1869, d: 1920, Occupation: m.Exer Mincey

+Exer Mincey (1872 - 1895) b: 1872, m: Bef. 1894, d: 1895, Occupation: m.C.J.Summerour

............6John Mark Summerour (1871 - 1939) b: 1871, d: 1939, Occupation: m.Lona Goss

+Lona Goss (1874 - 1939) b: 1874, d: 1939, Occupation: m.J.M.Summerour

+Louisa Roberts (1849 - 1898) b: 1849, m: Bef. 1879, d: 1898, Occupation: 2wWm.F.Summerour

............6Robert Summerour (1879 - 1959) b: 1879, d: 1959, Occupation: never married

6 Generation Descendant Report for Heinrich Henry Summerour

   +Florence N. Whitamore (1874 - 1963) b: 1874, m: Bef. 1902, d: 1963, Occupation: 3wWm.F.Summerour
- 6Richard Homer Summerour (1902 - 1959) b: 1902, d: 1959, Occupation: m.Gertie Ingram
  - +Gertie Ingram (1920 - 1974) b: 1920, m: Bef. 1935, d: 1974, Occupation: m.R.H.Summerour
- 6Susan Summerour (1903 - 1910) b: 1903, d: 1910, Occupation: died young
- 6Annie Lou Summerour (1904 - 1942) b: 1904, d: 1942, Occupation: m.Grady Stone
- 6Henry Clay Summerour (1906 - 1978) b: 1906, d: 1978, Occupation: m.Irma Seay
  - +Emily Irene Seay (1914 -) b: 1914, m: Bef. 1931, Occupation: m.Noel Summerour

....5John Henry Summerour (1854 - 1920) b: 1854 in GA, d: 1920, Occupation: m.Marg.Mathews
  +Margaret Matthews (1851 - 1914) b: 1851, m: Bef. 1874, d: 1914, Occupation: m.J.H.Summerour
- 6Julia Elaine Summerour (1874 - 1965) b: 1874, d: 1965, Occupation: m.Gold Dale
  - +Gold Dale (1871 - 1932) b: 1871, m: Bef. 1896, d: 1932, Occupation: m.J.E.Summerour
- 6William Franklin Summerour (1876 - 1940) b: 1876, d: 1940, Occupation: m.Flor.Gillespie
  - +Florence E. Gillespie (1891 -) b: 1891, m: Bef. 1914, Occupation: m.Wm.F.Summerour
- 6John Lafayette Summerour (1879 - 1925) b: 1879, d: 1925, Occupation: m1.Davis2.Reed
  - +Emma Davis (1875 - 1925) b: 1875, m: Bef. 1904, d: 1925, Occupation: m.J.L.Summerour
- 6Zed Williford Summerour (1881 - 1924) b: 1881, d: 1924, Occupation: m.Verdie Pinson
- 6Charles Henry Summerour (1883 - 1965) b: 1883, d: 1965, Occupation: m.Azzie Norrell
  - +Azzie Lee Norrell (1890 - 1971) b: 1890, m: Bef. 1909, d: 1971, Occupation: m.C.H.Summerour
- 6Pulaski Summerour (1883 - 1889) b: 1883, d: 1889, Occupation: died young
- 6Susan Summerour (1885 - 1885) b: 1885, d: 1885, Occupation: infant death
- 6Annie Louise Summerour (1889 - 1968) b: 1889, d: 1968, Occupation: m.John Dale
  - +John N. Dale m: Bef. 1909, Occupation: m.AnnieSummerour
- 6David Allen Summerour (1889 - 1968) b: 1889, d: 02 Jan 1968 in Aurora, Lumpkin Co., GA, Burial: Jan 1968 in Lumpkin Co., GA, Occupation: m.Eliz.Dale
  - +Elizabeth Dale (1890 - after 1968) b: 1890, m: Bef. 1907, d: Aft. 1968, Occupation: m.Dave Summerour
- 6Ameldia Viola Summerour (1891 -) b: 1891, Occupation: m.T.W.Rogers
- 6Kate Salome Summerour (1893 - 1979) b: 1893, d: 1979, Occupation: m.Van Woody

....5Charles Lafayette Summerour (1856 - 1919) b: 1856 in GA, d: 1919, Occupation: m.MattieBearden

............5Thomas Iverson Summerour (1859 - 1941) b: 15 Dec 1859 in Dawson, Georgia, USA, d: 15 Jun 1941
     +Sara L Thompson (- 1900) b: GA, m: Bef. 1890 in GA, d: 1900, Occupation: 1w.TI Summerour
...............6Mary Elizabeth Summerour (1891 -) b: 1891 in GA
...............6Ruth Summerour (1893 -) b: 1893 in GA, Occupation: m.Jasper Cagle
...............6Franklin Summerour (- 1915) b: GA, d: 1915, Occupation: m.Miss Conner
     +Mary Emmaline Dodd (1870 - 1964) b: 04 Sep 1870 in Lumpkin, Georgia, USA, m: Aft. 1900 in GA, d: 24 Apr 1964 in Dawson, Georgia, USA
...............6Katie Lee Louella Summerour (1903 - 1982) b: 17 Jan 1903, d: 01 Mar 1982, Occupation: w.J.E.Clayton
     +Joseph Enoch Clayton Slayton (1894 - 1970) b: 1894 in GA, m: Bef. 1923 in GA, d: 1970 in GA, Occupation: M.KLL.Summerour
............5Susan Theodocia Summerour (1861 - 1931) b: 1861 in GA, d: 1931, Occupation: no children
............5Zion Ezekiel Summerour (1865 - 1938) b: 1865 in GA, d: 1938
     +Loucindy Southern (1874 - 1950) b: 1874, m: Bef. 1895 in GA, d: 1950, Occupation: w.Zion Summerour
...............6Martha Loucindy Summerour (1895 - 1978) b: 1895 in GA, d: 1978, Occupation: m.E.ZekeWaters
...............6Daniel Joseph Summerour (1897 - 1955) b: 1897 in GA, d: 1955
...............6Mildred Marshall Summerour (1899 - 1978) b: 1899, d: 1978, Occupation: m.JamesRhindress
...............6Charles Henry Summerour (1903 -) b: 1903 in GA, Occupation: m.LillieAdamson
...............6Nurnil Grace Summerour (1905 -) b: 1905 in GA, Occupation: m.FrnklnSanders
...............6Kittie Sue Summerour (1909 -) b: 1909 in GA, Occupation: m.CarlosPierce
............5Jamus Robert Lee Summerour (1867 - 1936) b: 1867 in GA, d: 1936, Occupation: m.Sarah O.Rogers
............5Daniel Alexander Summerour (1869 - 1936) b: 1869 in GA, d: 1936, Occupation: m.Dora Brown
............5Beverly Nathaniel Summerour (1874 - 1949) b: 1874 in GA, d: 1949, Occupation: m.Amanda Mathews
     +Ameldia Spriggs (1832 - 1908) b: 05 Sep 1832 in Saluda Valley, Greenville, South Carolina, United States, m: 07 Oct 1847 in ,Lumpkin,Georgia,USA, d: 10 Oct 1908 in Dawson, Georgia, United States
............5Thomas Iverson Summerour (1859 - 1941) b: 15 Dec 1859 in Dawson County, Ga, d: 15 Jun 1941 in Dawson County, Ga
     +Mary Emmaline Dodd (1870 - 1964) b: 04 Sep 1870 in Lumpkin, Georgia, USA, d: 24 Apr 1964 in Dawson, Georgia, USA
...............6Katie Lee Louella Summerour (1903 - 1982) b: 17 Jan 1903 in Forsyth County, Georgia, d: 01 Mar 1982 in Dawsonville, Dawson, Georgia, United States
.........4Anna Maria Summerour b: GA, Occupation: m.AllenMathews
   +Allen Mathews
......3Catherine Summerour (about 1790 -) b: Abt. 1790 in NC

6 Generation   Descendant Report for Heinrich Henry Summerour

  +Tapster David Finger m: Bef. 1810 in Lincoln Co NC
.........4Susan Finger (1810 -) b: 1810 in Lincoln Co NC, Occupation: w>Geo.A.Ikard
  +George A. Ikard (1807 -) b: 1807
.........4Annie Finger (1812 -) b: 1812 in Lincoln Co., NC, Occupation: w>Anthony Ikard
  +Anthony Ikard (1815 -) b: 1815
.........4Frances Finger (1813 - 1886) b: 1813 in Lincoln Co NC, d: 1886, Occupation: w>James Kistler
  +James Kistler
.........4Malinda Finger (1815 - 1846) b: 1815 in Lincoln Co NC, d: 1846, Occupation: w>DrHnryThornton
  +Henry Thornton Occupation: Doctor
.........4Elizabeth Finger (1817 - 1843) b: 1817 in Lincoln Co NC, d: 1843, Occupation: w>Elisha Ramsour
  +Elisha Ramsour
.........4Sallie Finger (1821 - 1854) b: 1821 in Lincoln Co NC, d: 1854, Occupation: w>Wm.Henson
  +William Henson (1816 -) b: 1816
......3John Summerour (1792 - 1867) b: 1792 in Lincolnton, Lincoln Co, NC, d: 1867 in Between, Walton Co., GA, Burial: Smith Cemetery, Moore Farm, Walton Co., GA
 +Margaret "Peggy" Berry (1797 - 1875) b: 1797 in North Carolina, United States; 1880 US Census Walton Co GA - said born 1797, m: 22 Dec 1817 in Lincoln Co NC; marriage bond, d: 01 Jul 1875 in died bef 1876, Walton Co Georgia; bef 1876 Walton Co GA. per GA Tax Digest 1871-1876, son Berry administrator of her estate, i.e. she died before 1876. Her tombstone in Alcovy Cemetery says" Unkown Birth and Death Dates., Burial: Bold Springs, Walton County, Georgia, USA
.........4Ezekial Summerour (1818 - 1894) b: 15 Nov 1818 in North Carolina, United States, d: 19 Jul 1894 in Henagar, DeKalb Co., Alabama, USA; Burial: Unity Baptist Missionary Cemetery, Henagar, DeKalb Co., Alabama, USA, Burial: Henagar, DeKalb County, Alabama, USA
 +Sarah Jane Sartor (1832 - 1919) b: 05 Aug 1832 in Hall Co., Georgia, USA, m: 22 Nov 1849 in Georgia, USA, d: 26 Mar 1919 in Henagar, DeKalb Co., Alabama, USA; Burial: Unity Baptist Missionary Cemetery, Henagar, DeKalb Co., Alabama, USA, Burial: Henagar, DeKalb County, Alabama, USA
............5Margaret Elizabeth Summerour (1850 - 1929) b: 28 Aug 1850 in Gwinnett Co., Georgia, USA, d: 01 Jan 1929 in Albertville, Marshall Co., Alabama, USA, Burial: Albertville, Marshall County, Alabama, USA
 +James Marion Howard
...............6Mary Virginia Howard (1868 - 1954) b: 17 Jul 1868 in Henagar, DeKalb Co., Alabama, USA, d: 07 Mar 1954 in Oneonta, Blount Co., Alabama, USA; Burial: Oak Hill Cemetery, Oneonta, Blount Co., Alabama, USA
...............6Isaac William Howard (1870 - 1938) b: 17 Apr 1870 in Henagar, DeKalb Co., Alabama, USA, d: 19 Mar 1938 in Maysville, Madison Co., Alabama, USA

6 Generation   Descendant Report for Heinrich Henry Summerour

+James Marion Howard (1842 - 1924) b: 16 Mar 1842 in Bridgeport, Jackson Co., Alabama, USA; Born on a Thursday, in Hogjaw Valley, three and 1/2 miles east of Bridgeport, Alabama. This was about 2 1/2 miles from where his parents were married., m: 30 Aug 1867, d: 03 Feb 1924 in Albertville, Marshall Co., Alabama, USA

............6Ninnah Josephine Howard (1871 - 1966) b: 23 Nov 1871 in Henagar, DeKalb Co., Alabama, USA, d: 08 Oct 1966 in Chattanooga, Hamilton Co., Tennessee, USA

............6Marena Alice Howard (1873 - 1960) b: 22 Mar 1873 in Henagar, DeKalb Co., Alabama, USA, d: 19 Jul 1960

............6Malvina (Vina) Howard (1875 - 1957) b: 14 May 1875 in Henagar, DeKalb Co., Alabama, USA, d: 16 Sep 1957 in Albertville, Marshall Co., Alabama, USA; Burial: Memory Hill Cemetery, Albertville, Marshall Co., Alabama, USA, Burial: Albertville Memorial Cemetery, Albertville, Marshall Co., Alabama, USA

............6Georgia Etta Howard (1877 - 1949) b: 27 Mar 1877 in Henagar, DeKalb Co., Alabama, USA, d: 26 Sep 1949 in Birmingham, Jefferson Co., Alabama, USA, Occupation: 1940 in Montgomery, Montgomery Co., Alabama, USA; Supervisor, Dept. of Education

............6Benjamin Franklin Howard Sr. (1881 - 1954) b: 13 Jan 1881 in Henagar, DeKalb Co., Alabama, USA, d: 01 Apr 1954 in Albertville, Marshall Co., Alabama, USA

............6Joseph Marion Howard Sr. (1882 - 1946) b: 29 Oct 1882 in Henagar, DeKalb Co., Alabama, USA, d: 31 Oct 1946 in Chattanooga, Hamilton Co., Tennessee, USA; Burial: Chattanooga Memorial Park Cemetery

............6Willis Timmons Howard Sr. (1884 - 1965) b: 20 Nov 1884 in Henagar, DeKalb Co., Alabama, USA, d: 14 Mar 1965 in Fort McClellan, Calhoun Co., Alabama, USA

............6Ella Mildred Howard (1887 - 1979) b: 11 Mar 1887 in Henagar, DeKalb Co., Alabama, USA, d: 28 Sep 1979 in Greenville, Butler Co., Alabama, USA; Burial: Magnolia Cemetery, Greenville, Butler Co., Alabama, USA, Burial: Magnolia Cemetery, Butler Co., Alabama, USA

............6Nettie Viola Howard (1888 - 1972) b: 25 Dec 1888 in Henagar, DeKalb Co., Alabama, USA, d: 28 May 1972 in Albertville, Marshall Co., Alabama, USA

............6Walter Lucian Howard Sr. (1891 - 1981) b: 08 Apr 1891 in Henagar, DeKalb Co., Alabama, USA, d: Nov 1981 in Albertville, Marshall Co., Alabama, USA

............6Charlsie Miriam Howard (1894 - 1987) b: 26 Jun 1894 in Henagar, DeKalb Co., Alabama, USA, d: 07 Jan 1987 in Cleveland, Blount Co., Alabama, USA

.........5Mary SUMMEROUR (1853 - 1934) b: 28 Aug 1853 in Georgia, United States, d: 26 Feb 1934

.........5William Harrison "Henry" Summerour (1855 - 1936) b: 25 Dec 1855 in Alabama, United States, d: 04 Sep 1936 in Dekalb

+Laura Emma Moore (1858 - 1951) b: 09 Dec 1858 in DeKalb County, Alabama, d: 07 Sep 1951 in DeKalb County Alabama, USA

............6Della Jane summerour (1890 -) b: 1890 in Alabama

.........5Cynthia Caroline Summerour (1859 - 1952) b: 10 Nov 1859, d: 25 Aug 1952

.........5Caroline Summerour (about 1861 - 1952) b: Abt. 1861 in Alabama, d: 25 Aug 1952

.........5Sarah Ellen SUMMEROUR (1865 - 1959) b: 08 May 1865, d: 23 Feb 1959

.........5Henry Summerour

.........4John Summerour Jr. 1823 (1823 - 1865) b: 03 May 1823 in NC, d: 1865 in Walton, Georgia, USA, Burial: Old Alcovy Cemetery, Bold Springs GA. Walton County
    +Nancy Vineyard (1831 - 1857) b: 1831 in Georgia; 1850USCN-WaltonCoGA:ag 19, i.e. born circa 183, m: 19 Dec 1848 in Gwinnett, Georgia, USA, d: 1857 in Walton, Georgia, United States; died in childbirth: George Stephen Summerour.
............5James Berry1852 Summerour (1852 - 1925) b: 22 Jun 1852 in Walton Co GA, USA, d: 25 Apr 1925 in Lindley, Walton, Georgia, United States
    +M Elora (about 1863 -) b: Abt. 1863 in Georgia
...............6Vergia Summerour (1911 -) b: 04 Jan 1911
    +Martha Tuck (1862 - 1911) b: 1862 in Georgia, m: 1890, d: 1911
...............6S Ethel Summerour (1892 -) b: 1892, Occupation: m.JohnBriscoe
    +John Briscoe (1880 - 1950) b: 1880, m: Bef. 1919, d: 1950
...............6J Mack Summerour (about 1895 -) b: Abt. 1895 in Georgia, Occupation: m.Nell Patrick
...............6Cora Lou Summerour (1898 -) b: 1898, Occupation: m.Troy Smith
...............6Ina Summerour (about 1902 - 1995) b: Abt. 1902 in Georgia, d: 10 Jul 1995 in Clarke, Georgia, USA, Occupation: m.Emory Queen
    +Emory Queen m: Bef. 1930
...............6James B. Summerour Jr. (1907 -) b: 1907, Occupation: never married
    +Lizzie
    +Lizzie Summerour (about 1870 -) b: Abt. 1870 in Georgia
    +Sarah L. Smith (1853 - 1891) b: 1853, d: 1891, Occupation: w>J.B.Summerour
............5William Franklin Summerour (1855 - 1925) b: 1855 in Walton Co., GA, d: 1925 in GA, USA
    +Emma Graham (1865 - 1922) b: 1865, d: 1922, Occupation: w>Wm.F.Summerour
...............6Jessie Summerour (1888 -) b: 1888, Occupation: w>H.C.Forester
...............6Ester Summerour (1895 -) b: 1895, Occupation: m.L.R.Jones
...............6Robert Daniel Summerour (1898 -) b: 1898, Occupation: m.Alice Jones
    +Alice Jones (1901 -) b: 1901, m: Bef. 1921
...............6Luddie Summerour Occupation: m.R.Eddleman
    +M. Towler
............5George Stephen Summerour (1857 - 1934) b: 1857 in Walton Co., GA, d: 11 Jun 1934 in Georgia
    +Mary Jurdie Smith (1861 - 1934) b: 1861, d: 1934
...............6Martha Bush Summerour (1881 -) b: 1881, Occupation: m.Marion Maynard
...............6John N. Summerour (1883 -) b: 1883, Occupation: mBirdieEtheridge
...............6Mary Fanny Summerour (1885 - 1928) b: 1885, d: 1928, Occupation: m.ErastusMoore
...............6James W. Summerour (1888 -) b: 1888, Occupation: m.BertaRoberts
...............6George William Summerour (1891 - 1969) b: 1891, d: 1969, Occupation: m.JesseCaldwell
    +Jesse Caldwell m: Bef. 1919
...............6Oscar Elijah Summerour (1893 - 1944) b: 03 Aug 1893 in Georgia, d: 09 Aug 1944 in Barrow, Georgia

6 Generation   Descendant Report for Heinrich Henry Summerour

................+Lillie Belle Robinson (1894 - 1968) b: 1894, m: Georgia, USA, d: 1968 in Georgia, USA
...............6Ella Mae Summerour (1897 -) b: 1897, Occupation: m.ClydeEskridge
........+Mary Carter (1833 -) b: May 1833 in Georgia, USA, m: 07 Dec 1858 in Oglethorpe, Georgia, USA
............5JS Summerour (1858 -) b: 1858 in Georgia, United States
............5Elizabeth J Summerour (1860 -) b: 1860 in Georgia, United States
............5Ezekial Jefferson Summerour (1861 - 1930) b: 30 May 1861 in Georgia, United States, d: 10 Jul 1930 in Georgia, United States
................+Dora Bradford (about 1877 - 1966) b: Abt. 1877 in Georgia, m: Bef. 1907, d: 1966, Occupation: w>ZekeSummerour
...............6E. J. (Zeke) Summerour Jr. (about 1908 - 1978) b: Abt. 1908 in Georgia, d: 1978
................+irma cochran (1905 -) b: 1905
...............6Clarice L. Summerour (1914 -) b: 1914, Occupation: m.Mr.Chambers
............5Nancy Summerour (1863 - 1924) b: 03 Oct 1863 in Georgia, d: 10 Sep 1924 in Monroe, Walton County, Georgia, Burial: Monroe, Walton County, Georgia, USA
................+William Pierce Bearden (1847 - 1925) b: 02 Dec 1847 in Georgia, United States, m: 1880, d: 21 Jan 1925 in GA; Age: 77, Burial: Monroe, Walton County, Georgia, USA
...............6Hettie Bearden (1875 - 1957) b: 1875 in Georgia, d: 1957 in Atlanta, Fulton county, Georgia
...............6Pearl Beardin (about 1877 -) b: Abt. 1877 in Georgia
...............6Willie Bearden (1881 - 1955) b: 1881, d: 1955
...............6William S Bearden (1881 -) b: Jul 1881 in Walton, Georgia, United States
...............6Mary R Bearden (1884 -) b: Jan 1884 in Walton, Georgia, United States
...............6Mary B. Bearden (1884 - 1935) b: 1884, d: 1935, Occupation: m.Mr.Clower
...............6Della B. Bearden (1886 -) b: 1886, Occupation: m.CharlesWooley
...............6Florence O'Della Bearden (1886 - 1976) b: 26 Jun 1886 in Walton County, Georgia, d: 18 May 1976 in Atlanta, Fulton, Georgia, United States of America; Age: 89 Years
...............6John Richard Bearden (1888 - 1968) b: 1888, d: 1968
...............6John Richard Bearden (1889 - 1967) b: 03 May 1889 in Monroe, Walton, Georgia, United States, d: 02 Feb 1967 in Monroe, Walton, Georgia, United States
...............6James Tom Bearden (1891 - 1931) b: 1891, d: 1931
...............6James Bearden (1892 -) b: Mar 1892 in Walton, Georgia, United States
.........4Berry J Summerour (1829 - 1905) b: 10 Nov 1829 in Walton, Georgia, USA, Military Exper.: 07 May 1862 in Social Circle, Walton Co. GA ; CSA: Company D, 2nd GA Calvary, Pvt in Capt. grout's Calvery Co, Lawton's Regt. / Wounded wintr 1872TN, Stones River w Gen. Braxton Bragg, dismounted cavalry, wagon train., d: 10 Feb 1905 in Selma, Montague, Texas, United States, Occupation: Farmer
............+Mary L. "Polly" Vineyard (1832 - 1922) b: 19 Aug 1832 in GA, per 1860 GA CN-+Death Certific-1922, m: 26 Nov 1850 in Gwinnett Co GA; by John W. Matthes: GA Marriage Records from Select Counties, 1828-1978, d: 29 Jul 1922 in Selma, Montague, Texas, United States

6 Generation   Descendant Report for Heinrich Henry Summerour

............5Mary Livina Summerour (1854 - 1947) b: 22 Mar 1854 in Walton County, Georgia, d: 20 Nov 1947 in Whitesboro, TX; 1900 USCN-Stated mother of NO chldren, None dead., Occupation: m.Mr.Palmer
   +G. W. Palmer (1845 - after 1900) b: Mar 1845 in Georgia, m: 1874, d: Aft. 1900
............5Elizabeth Summerour (1855 -) b: 1855 in GA, d: Walton, Georgia, United States
   +Tom Paine
............6Willy Paine
............6Jesse Paine
............5Susan Mae Summerour (1859 - 1926) b: 14 Apr 1859 in Walton Co GA, d: 06 Dec 1926 in Sunset, Montague, Texas, United States, Occupation: Farmwife
   +Thomas W. Johnigan (1863 -) b: 1863 in TX, USA, m: 26 Dec 1881 in TX, d: Texas
   +Porter Kalvin Wininger (1855 - 1951) b: 14 Jul 1855 in Hawkins CoTN, m: 28 Mar 1885 in Montague Co. TX, d: 13 Oct 1951 in Smith, Texas, USA; Age: 96, Burial: 13 Oct 1951 in Brushy Cemetery, Bowie, Monteague Co., TX, Occupation: Farmer
............6Cora Mae Wininger (1887 - 1977) b: 20 Dec 1887 in Sunset, Montague, Texas, USA, d: 16 Aug 1977 in Duncan, Stephens, OK, Occupation: Farmwife
   +John Robert Moore (1880 - 1966) b: 01 Apr 1880 in Charleston, Franklin Co AR, m: 1905 in TX, d: 29 Jun 1966 in Duncan, Stephens Co., OK, Burial: 1966 in Duncan Municipal Cemetery, Duncan, Stephens, OK
............6Lela Elizabeth Wininger (1889 - 1982) b: 24 Aug 1889 in Sunset, Montague, Texas, United States, d: 05 Nov 1982 in Vallejo, Solano, California, United States, Burial: 1982 in Vallejo, Solano Co CA, Occupation: Homemaker
   +Marion Lee Moore (1882 - 1960) b: 23 Jul 1882 in Charleston, Franklin, Arkansas, United States, m: 22 Sep 1907 in Park Springs, Wise TX, d: 21 Jun 1960 in Vallejo, Solano, California, US Age 77, Occupation: 1918 ; Railroad Foreman, at Rock Island RR from age 18(1900), till it downsized in 1918, when he was discharged., Occupation: 1920 ; Teamster -, Occupation: 1920 in Burkburnette, Witchita Co. TX; Rock Island Railroad, Section Hand, Occupation: 1930 ; Odd Jobs, Occupation: Apr 1940 in Maguire, Tilman Co OK ; WPA Carpenter: $200 year, Occupation: 1942 ; Pipefitter at Mare Island Naval Yard until retired at 65 (1947), Occupation: 1940 APR 1; Maguire, Tillman Co OK -$200 yearWPA Carpenter
............6Lavana Angeline Wininger (1891 - 1987) b: 13 Mar 1891 in Montague Co. TX, d: 24 Jan 1987 in Stephens, Oklahoma, United States, Occupation: Farmwife
   +H. Frank Thomas (before 1891 - 1967) b: Bef. 1891, m: 21 Oct 1906 in Montague Co TX, d: 15 Jun 1967 in Waurika, OK
   +Frank Thomas (about 1890 -) b: Abt. 1890, m: Bef. 1907 in TX
............6Clementine "Clemie" W. Wininger (1893 - 1985) b: 20 Jun 1893 in Sunset, Montague, Texas, USA, d: 31 Jan 1985 in Orange, California, Occupation: Housewife

6 Generation Descendant Report for Heinrich Henry Summerour

+William Newton "Will" Moore Sr. (1868 - 1946) b: 25 May 1868 in Hot Springs, Garland, Arkansas, USA, m: 29 Sep 1912 in Arkansas, United States, d: 05 Mar 1946 in Burkburnett, Wichita, Texas, USA; Age: 78, Burial: 10 Mar 1946 in Burkburnett, Wichita, Texas, USA; Burkburnett Cemetery- Plot: 14-30-3, Occupation: Bet. 1890–1925 in Burkburnett, Wichita, Texas; Retd Oil Field Wker-Farm

...........6Oscar Levi Wininger (1896 - 1971) b: 13 Jan 1896 in Bowie, Texas, USA, d: Dec 1971 in TX

+Exia Capps (- 1981) d: 05 Jan 1981 in Bexar Co., TX

...........6William Wininger (1898 - 1956) b: Apr 1898 in Montague Co. TX, d: 20 Dec 1956 in Shreveport, Bossier, Louisiana, United States

...........6Athel Wininger (1899 - 1978) b: 08 Dec 1899 in Montague Co. TX, d: 07 Jun 1978 in Victoria Co. TX 77901

...........6John Elgar (John Ike) Wininger (1904 - 1945) b: 05 Jun 1904 in Sunset, Montague, Texas, USA, d: 11 May 1945 in Bowie, Texas, United States; Age 40, Burial: 1945 in Bowie, Montague County, Texas, USA; Brushy Cemetery, Occupation: Overton, Smith, Texas; Pipe Line Worker

+Velva Deliska Doering Harris (1908 - 2004) b: 10 Jan 1908 in Findley, Ohio, United States, m: Sunset, Montague, Texas, United States, d: 12 Aug 2004 in Springville, Tulare, California, United States of America, Burial: 2004 in Tipton, Tulare, California, United States; Tipton-Pixley Cemetery - Plot: B.1-L.45-G.5

........5James Berry_1864 Summerour (1864 - 1948) b: 02 Sep 1864 in Walton, Georgia, United States, d: 22 Jul 1948 in Amarillo, Potter, Texas, United States

+Henrietta Melvina Dawson (1871 - 1948) b: 25 Jan 1871 in Cooke, Texas, USA, m: 1888, d: 22 Jul 1948 in Amarillo, Potter, Texas, United States, Burial: Clarendon, Donley, Texas, USA; Citizens Cemetery

...........6Lillie M Summerow (1888 - 1977) b: 18 Sep 1888 in Texas, d: 05 Jun 1977 in Amarillo, Potter, Texas, USA; Age: 88

+Vernon Bagwell (about 1879 -) b: Abt. 1879 in Tennessee

...........6Lucy Pearl Summerow (1891 - 1989) b: Feb 1891 in Texas, d: 30 Sep 1989 in Childress, Texas, USA

+Cyrus Cope (1884 - 1956) b: 02 Nov 1884 in Texas, USA, m: 30 Nov 1910 in Texas, USA, d: Jun 1956 in Texas, USA

...........6Equilla Summerow (1893 -) b: Oct 1893 in Texas

...........6James Elmer Summerour (1896 - 1969) b: 05 Apr 1896 in Indian Territory ; now Oklahoma, USA, d: 29 Nov 1969 in Dalhart, Harrison, Texas, USA; Age: 73, Burial: Memorial Park Cemetery, Dalhart, Dallam, Texas, USA

+Edith Dorothy Pronger (1906 - 1995) b: 10 May 1906 in England, d: 11 Sep 1995 in Dalhart, Hartley, Texas, USA, Burial: Memorial Park Cemetery, Dalhart, Dallam, Texas, USA

...........6Henry Floyd Summerour (1899 - 1988) b: 18 Jan 1899 in Texas, d: 24 Aug 1988 in Taylor, Texas; Age at Death: 89, Burial: Clyde, Callahan County, Texas, USA

+Bessie Lee McKinley (1906 - 1985) b: 14 Apr 1906 in Oplin, Callahan County, Texas, USA, d: 14 Nov 1985 in Baird, Callahan, Texas, USA

...........6William A Summerour (1904 -) b: 1904 in Texas

6 Generation   Descendant Report for Heinrich Henry Summerour

    +Lucy Dawson (1868 - 1958) b: 05 Nov 1868 in Grafton, Wise, Texas, USA, m: 1895 in Texas, d: 21 Feb 1958 in Amarillo, Potter, Texas, USA; Age: 89, Burial: Claude, Armstrong County, Texas, USA

............6Lillie Summerour (1889 -) b: 1889 in TX

............6James Elmer Summerour (1896 - 1969) b: 05 Apr 1896 in Indian Territory ; now Oklahoma, USA, d: 29 Nov 1969 in Dalhart, Harrison, Texas, USA; Age: 73, Burial: Memorial Park Cemetery, Dalhart, Dallam, Texas, USA

    +Edith Dorothy Pronger (1906 - 1995) b: 10 May 1906 in England, d: 11 Sep 1995 in Dalhart, Hartley, Texas, USA, Burial: Memorial Park Cemetery, Dalhart, Dallam, Texas, USA

............6Henry F Summerour (about 1899 -) b: Abt. 1899 in Texas

............6Lucy Summerour (1904 -) b: 1904 in TX

............6Equilla Summerour (1904 -) b: 1904 in TX

............6William R Summerour (about 1904 -) b: Abt. 1904 in Texas

............6Virgia D Summerour (about 1911 -) b: Abt. 1911 in Texas

.........5William D. Summerour (1867 - 1930) b: 26 Jun 1867 in Walton Co., GA, d: 03 Jul 1930 in Montague Co., TX

.........5John Allen Summerour (1869 - 1968) b: 29 Oct 1869 in Monroe, Walton Co., GA, d: 11 May 1968 in Loma Linda, San Bernadino Co., CA

  +Sarah Eliz. Leanora Rozell

............6Inez Catherine Summerour (1911 - 1962) b: 20 Nov 1911 in NM, d: 03 Dec 1962 in Bell Gardens, Los Angeles, CA

    +Lester Sisk

............6Ruby Betheljean Summerour (1914 -) b: 21 Nov 1914 in Lake Arthur, Chaves, NM

    +Ira Jacoway m: 1933 in Oceanside, San Diego, CA

     +George Alexander Strahan (1912 - 1971) b: 06 Aug 1912 in Yonkers, Westchester, NY, m: 23 Mar 1936 in Los Angeles, Los Angeles Co., CA, d: 05 Feb 1971 in Redlands, San Bernadino, CA

  +Julia Neece (1876 -) b: Mar 1876 in GA, m: 24 Dec 1894 in Montague Co TX

............6Marion Summerour (1895 - about 1964) b: Dec 1895 in Montague Co TX, d: Abt. 1964 in Kansas City, MO

............6Lee Summerour (1898 -) b: Dec 1898 in Elkcity, Roger Mills, OK

.........5George W. Summerour (1873 - 1910) b: 18 Feb 1873 in Walton Co., GA, d: 19 Jan 1910 in Montague Co. TX, Burial: Jan 1910 in Selma Cemetery, Montague Co., TX

......4Cynthia Summerour (1830 - 1890) b: 1830, d: 1890 in Milledgeville, Baldwin, Georgia, USA, Occupation: w>Mr.Pannell

  +Wiley Panel (1826 -) b: 1826, m: Georgia, USA; Y;Y;Y, d: Y

.........5Mary Ann PANNELL (1842 -) b: 1842 in Georgia, USA, d: Y

.........5Margaret PANNELL (1847 -) b: 1847 in Georgia, USA, d: Y

......4Elizabeth Summerour (1832 - 1915) b: 1832 in Walton, Georgia, United States, d: 15 Feb 1915 in Newton, Georgia, United States; Buried in Macedonia Cemetery Oxford GA

  +Joe George

6 Generation   Descendant Report for Heinrich Henry Summerour

.........4William Summerour (1834 - after 1850) b: 1834 in GA, d: Aft. 1850 in Walton Co., GA census 1850

.........4Margaret Summerour (1836 - after 1850) b: 1836 in GA, d: Aft. 1850 in 1850 Walton, GA census., Occupation: m.Rufus Self

+Henry Briscoe

.........4Daniel Summerour c. 1827 b: Walton Co., GA

......3Mary Summerour (about 1794 -) b: Abt. 1794 in NC

+David Finger (1794 - 1871) b: 1794, m: Bef. 1820, d: 1871

.........4Levi Finger (1820 -) b: 1820, Occupation: M.Ann Hallman

.........4Henry Finger (1822 -) b: 1822, Occupation: m.Mary Forney

.........4Solomon Finger (1827 -) b: 1827, Occupation: m.NancyCarpenter

.........4Sarah 'Sally' Finger (1828 -) b: 1828, Occupation: m.Col.H.A.Forney

.........4Susan Finger

.........4James Franklin Finger

......3Tapster Jacob Summerour (about 1801 -) b: Abt. 1801 in NC

+Barbara Hallman (1801 -) b: 1801

.........4Elizabeth Summerour (1832 - 1915) b: 1832 in Walton, Georgia, United States, d: 15 Feb 1915 in Newton, Georgia, United States; Buried in Macedonia Cemetery Oxford GA

+Joe George

.........4Margaret Summerour (1836 - after 1850) b: 1836 in GA, d: Aft. 1850 in 1850 Walton, GA census., Occupation: m.Rufus Self

+Henry Briscoe

.........4Adaline Summerour Occupation: m.Wm.Phovey

.........4Susan Summerour Occupation: m.Cany Harthoke

.........4Rochelle Summerour Occupation: m.MiltonCampbell

.........4Rosanna Summerour Occupation: m.DavidHaulbrook

.........4Mary Summerour

......3Anna Summerour (1805 -) b: 1805 in NC

+Lewis Keener (1805 - 1904) b: 1805, m: Bef. 1842, d: 1904

.........4Mary E. Keener Occupation: m.Milton Goodson

.........4Susan R. Keener Occupation: m.Andrew Link

.........4William A. Keener Occupation: m.SalinaGoodson

.........4Henry F. Keener

......3Susan Summerour (about 1806 - 1895) b: Abt. 1806 in NC, d: 1895

+Jonas Finger m: Bef. 1823

.........4Salome Finger

......3Sally Summerour (- about 1896) b: NC, d: Abt. 1896 in NC

...2John Summerour (1765 -) b: 1765

...2Solomon Summerour (1768 -) b: 1768